THE
Birth Partner
HANDBOOK

Everything You Need to Know for a
Healthy, Positive Birth Experience

C A R L   J O N E S

sourcebooks

Published by Sourcebooks, Inc.
P.O. Box 4410, Naperville, Illinois 60567-4410
(630) 961-3900
Fax: (630) 961-2168
www.sourcebooks.com

Library of Congress Cataloging-in-Publication Data

Jones, Carl.
   The birth partner handbook : everything you need to know for a healthy, positive birth experience / by Carl Jones.
      p. cm.
   1. Childbirth. 2. Fathers. 3. Natural childbirth—Coaching. I. Title.
RG651.J66 2010
618.4—dc22
                           2010003100

Printed and bound in the United States of America.
VP 10 9 8 7 6 5 4 3 2 1

CONTENTS

· · · · · · · · · · ·

Chapter One

THE BIRTH PARTNER

If you are well prepared for labor, you are worth your weight in Demerol. There is nothing that can ease the laboring mother's fear and soothe her pain like a supportive childbirth companion. Nothing can more easily help her to experience a joyful birth.

I have asked scores of women, "What helped you most during labor?" Their answers include "My partner," "I could have never done it without my husband," "I was not alone during labor. My mother was with me every minute. It made all the difference in the world for me," and "During many hard-to-handle contractions, my husband was indispensable to me. His soothing voice, caring smile, and warm, supporting arms meant the difference between manageable contractions and being dominated by pain." Another woman said, "I was terrified of labor. I couldn't imagine anything short of general anesthesia getting me through the ordeal. But Roger was amazing. Just being by my side and holding my hand, he helped me focus during many difficult contractions. I labored medication free and have never regretted it!"

"Like most women I know, I was afraid of labor," recalled Tess about the birth of her first child. "I had my doubts about my husband, Larry, being able to help me. When it came right down to the wire, he was as nervous as I was. But he was wonderful during labor! Just standing by my side, walking with me, holding me when I lay down, evaporated the sting of the most difficult contractions and set my whirling mind at peace."

So you are going to attend a labor. You are about to embark on one of the greatest and most rewarding adventures life has to offer: the birth of a child. Nothing is more exciting that witnessing the entrance of a child into the world. It is especially miraculous when it is your own child being born. "I can't believe what a thrill being at the birth was for me," said Jared about the birth of his baby girl. "It was such a high. I was so elated I could hardly speak. I would recommend [that] every father get as well prepared for labor as possible. The better prepared he is, the better he can take away his mate's pain. The better prepared he is, the more likely he will be swept away by the ecstasy of birth."

While you enjoy the birth, you can reduce the mother's fear and pain as you maximize her joy in the childbearing miracle. No form of pain medication is as safe or as effective as her childbirth companion's labor support. As a companion, you can spell the difference between a nightmare of agony and confusion and an event always to be remembered with joy. There are numerous benefits to the mother who has a supportive birth partner. The childbirth companion can help the mother relax, reduce her fear, alleviate her pain, reduce the length of labor, lessen the chance of a Cesarean section, reduce the chance of childbirth complications, minimize the need for medical intervention, help the mother make a smooth transition to parenthood, result in more successful breast-feeding, and reduce the chance of postpartum depression.

In an oft-quoted medical study, Dr. John Kennel and his colleagues discovered that women who had a supportive companion with them during labor had shorter labors, developed fewer complications, and experienced significantly less pain than women who did not have supportive companions. The mothers with companions also stroked, smiled at, and talked to their newborns significantly more than did those without companions.

Why does effective labor support make such a tremendous difference in the mother's experience of childbirth? Largely because the mother is very vulnerable and open to suggestion during labor. The childbirth companion's presence helps keep the mother focused on coping with her contractions while easing the pain of labor. And the childbirth companion is able to give the mother positive suggestions that actually reduce her pain in labor and the length of labor. The childbirth companion can also help the mother relax. Labor is more painful when the mother is tense, but a relaxed woman is able to labor with less discomfort. In addition, the childbirth companion's practical help increases the effectiveness of labor-coping techniques, such as guided imagery.

The support that a mother receives during labor molds her entire experience. As mentioned, throughout labor, the mother is vulnerable, highly sensitive, and easily influenced by suggestion—especially the positive suggestions of a loving word or touch. Just being by her side helps her surrender to rather than fight the forces to give birth to her child.

Whatever your relationship with the mother, you can provide something that her physician or midwife and nurses cannot—the comfort and support of someone she knows and trusts. A familiar face, a kind word, a caressing touch can mean more than any drug or analgesia. Labor is undeniably painful at times, and it is not like any other pain. The pain of being in labor responds to emotional and physical support. The well-supported mother often experiences her labor as richly rewarding. "It was the most rewarding experience of my life," recalls Jamie about the birth of her first child. "Andrew and I did it together. I felt like I was plugged into something greater than myself. I had pain, yes. But the pain was nothing compared to the immense joy that labor brought. Of course giving birth was joyful. But I am talking about all of labor. It was a rewarding experience that I will never, ever forget."

Women frequently report that they could have never gone through labor as confidently without their husband, friend, or other childbirth companion. For example, one new mother, Anna, said, "I can't imagine how I could ever have gone through labor without my friend Cheryl present. Just being with me, she gave me the strength I needed." June, the mother of a newborn girl, recalled, "I feared being alone during labor. I felt too vulnerable, too easily upset to be by myself. Jim was with me throughout labor, from the very first contraction to the first hours after the baby was born. His presence meant everything to me. I was able to concentrate on getting through labor rather than being frightened and alone. Every father should attend the birth of his child. Lacking the father present, the mother should recruit a family member or close friend to help her through labor. If she can't find someone she trusts, she should honestly consider hiring someone: a professional labor support person or childbirth companion."

Anyone—father, friend, or family member, male or female—can help a mother through labor. Andrea, a first-time mother, remarked, "My friend Janet was everything to me. I don't know how I would have coped with labor without her. She helped me relax and talked me through contractions. When labor got rough, the look in her eyes said to me, 'I've done this before and so can you.' And that gave me confidence."

But you may feel that you know nothing about childbirth or you may be nervous if you have never attended a birth. Rest assured that most people who assist a woman through labor have never previously attended a birth. You don't need a world of knowledge to help a woman through labor. Many childbirth companions have never even seen a videotape of a birth. Most fathers know only what they have learned in childbirth classes. Some never even go to childbirth classes. But these fathers are still able to reduce the mother's fear and pain dramatically. Andy, a new father who helped his partner through labor, said, "I didn't know very much about childbirth besides what I had read. I was nervous about helping my wife, Linda, through labor. I only knew that my presence during labor meant a great deal to her. I didn't attend childbirth classes but I practiced guided imagery with Linda. When it came time for the real thing, I was able to lead her through an imagery exercise and I was just able to cuddle her when contractions waxed strong. She labored smoothly without the use of pain relief medication and had a beautiful birth."

How can you help when you don't have a shred of confidence about your role during labor? It is normal for you to feel anxious and unsure of yourself. The chapters ahead will share with you all you need to know to reduce fear and pain greatly and to enjoy the childbearing miracle to the fullest. Understanding labor will let you know what to expect about your partner's changing behavior and state of mind—and you can help her immensely.

"Bill read accurate descriptions of the mother's changing

behavior," recalled Cherie, the mother of three children. "He knew what to expect and how best to meet my changing needs. He was immensely helpful during labor. Just being there with me, accepting my behavior as normal, caused me to feel that labor was something I could take in stride. And I sailed through labor because of that. Without his presence and acceptance, I would surely have been lost."

If you are a secondary birth partner, attending the birth with the father or other primary birth partner, you can help both the mother and her partner cope, and you can help the primary birth partner better support the mother. Jackie, a new mother of a baby girl, remembered, "My friend Sharon kept pouring hot water over me in the tub. This helped a lot when contractions were really intense. Meanwhile, my husband, Brandon, held my hand and kept up eye contact."

Some single mothers and couples hire a trained childbirth companion, called a doula, to give primary labor support. In this case, the partner, relative, or friend has an important role to play in giving secondary labor support. The secondary support person can rub the mother's back, make her comfortable, give emotional encouragement, and provide the assurance of a familiar face. There are innumerable ways you can assist the mother or the primary birth partner. (For specific suggestions, see chapter 4, "Helping Her Every Step of the Way: Early Labor" and chapter 5, "Helping Her Every Step of the Way: Active Labor.")

However you prepare for birth and whether you are the primary or secondary labor support person, bear in mind that you are not a coach. Some childbirth educators used to use the term *labor coach* to describe the birth partner's role in labor. But *labor coach* does not adequately describe what the childbirth companion does. Fortunately, the majority of childbirth educators no longer use this term, but nonetheless it has stuck for some people. If someone calls you a coach, correct him or her. The coach belongs on the football field. You are there to nurture the laboring mother, to give her emotional and physical support, and to help her surrender to the childbearing miracle.

ESPECIALLY FOR FATHERS

Today, almost all expectant fathers attend the birth of their child, and obstetricians and other health-care professionals welcome fathers during prenatal appointments and during labor. For the most part, childbirth classes are for couples. Most women want their partners by their side during the life-altering hours of labor.

Every expectant father can help his partner in ways no one else can. No one cares for the laboring woman as her partner does. Aside from the mother herself, no one else is more deeply involved in her labor than the father of the child. For the father, no task is more rewarding that helping your partner through labor and knowing that your touch can ease her pain. And nothing is as satisfying or as utterly overwhelming as participating in the birth of your own child. "If there was ever one turning point in my life," recalled Toby, a new father, "this was it. Being there was the greatest joy I have ever known."

Of the birth of his son Damien, Brandon said, "It was the most important day of my life. Words can't describe it!" Derek, a new father to a baby girl, commented, "It was an intense experience. We were fully prepared for the birth and knew precisely what to expect. But when the time came, a flood of emotion came over me. I wanted to cry aloud. I wanted to tell the whole world our story—Sara and I gave birth together!"

A father's facial expressions during birth reveal the story unfolding. Powerful emotions pulse through his body, his eyes fill with tears, and his mouth tightens and then quivers into a wide smile. Considering the deep pride and elation that sweep through a father when he first gazes into the eyes of his child, and the incomparable image of family unity when mother, father, and newborn embrace after birth, it's easy to understand why so many men speak of their child's birth as the most sacred event of their lives.

At the birth of my first child, I felt as if I were standing on the threshold of mystery, privileged to witness a miracle as great as the creation of the earth. I had planned to take pictures for our family album, but at the time, photography was the last thing on my mind. Jan, my wife, was utterly beside herself. The expression on her face as she bore down with contractions was one of pure pleasure.

I could see a bit of the baby's head in the birth canal—a mere spot of wet, matted hair. Jan bore down fiercely. She gripped me so powerfully in her arms that I staggered against the bed and nearly fell on top of her. The climax was upon us. The baby moved downward in the birth canal and the head became larger and larger. I trembled. For a brief moment I was so afraid that I wanted to hide my face in my hands. It was all too wonderful to believe. Suddenly Jan gripped me in a wild, passionate embrace. The head was born. A few seconds more and the body slipped out easily.

I stood back for a moment, shaking with excitement. In the dimly lit room, Jan's face glowed and her blond hair fell in radiant folds. She looked like a goddess. As she lifted our son to her breast, her whole body radiated with ecstasy. She smiled. I took the baby into my arms and we locked eyes, my son and I. Waves of indescribable feeling swept down and up my spine.

"We are pregnant" is a common expression. It is more than a cute turn of phrase. Today, pregnancy means more than the growth of a baby in the uterus. It connotes the state of expectant parenthood that both mother and father share. The father may even have a feeling that a baby is on the way or share his partner's prenatal symptoms, such as morning sickness, gas pains, inexplicable weight gain, and constipation. These symptoms have been reported in fathers for centuries and are known as couvade syndrome (*couvade* comes from the French verb *couver*, which means "to hatch" or "brood"). Couvade syndrome represents a sharing of the childbearing experience on a deep psychological level.

The father of the child has a twofold role during labor. First is to witness the birth of the child and enjoy the childbearing miracle. Kenny, a new father, explained that watching the birth of his child was the most exhilarating thing he ever experienced and that a father can't know that feeling without being there. Second is to reduce the mother's fear and pain, and help her to enjoy childbearing to the fullest. Pamela, the mother of two children, found that her husband's presence during her second labor was as valuable as it was during her first, much-longer labor. "I wanted to have David next to me so I could hold on to him when I needed to," she said. Cammie, who labored for 3 days with her first child, said of her husband Steve: "We were a team. He helped me keep my breathing relaxed and easy, applied pressure to my lower back when I had back pain, and helped me relax. His help was invaluable."

Helping the mother relax and reducing her discomfort are not the only benefits of a father's presence during labor. According to a study conducted by Drs. Peterson, Mehl, and Leiderman, fathers who attend the birth of their child adapt more quickly to their nurturing role with the infant. The first moment with the newborn is the most dramatic part of childbirth for many fathers. As Paul, a new father of a boy says, "The moment we locked eyes, my newborn son and I, was even more awesome than witnessing the birth. I felt electric energy all through my body. This was the beginning of father-son attachment and I enjoyed it thoroughly."

Don't worry about the fact that you will never go through labor yourself. You don't need personal experience to make a difference. As the father of the child, because of your special relationship with the mother, you may even be a more effective labor support companion than her friends and relatives. "I didn't know the first thing about labor," recalled J. T. about the birth of his first child. "I could sense the sheer power my words and touch had on Marion. I was able to reduce her fear and lessen her pain. I was instrumental in making our birth the number-one experience of our lives."

You are bound to be anxious about the birth. This is especially true if you have never seen a birth and the upcoming one is the first you'll be attending. Many expectant fathers feel anxious about being with their partners in labor and seeing the actual birth. Some imagine childbirth as a medical event during which they will only feel awkward and in the way. Tessa's husband Ron doesn't want to attend the birth of his child because he feels that he can't "take it." This is not an uncommon reaction. But few fathers regret having shared the birth experience with their partners. They learn that giving birth can be the most creative and positive experience in their lives—hard work, yes, but an event of triumph and joy.

"I didn't want to attend the birth of my child at first," said Don, the father of a baby girl, "but I was in for a great surprise…I was fully enjoying every minute of the birth. It was the most exciting part of labor. I will always remember attending the birth of my daughter with joy."

Dominic was even more hesitant. His wife, Maria, was in labor with her third child. Dominic stood by her side in the labor room. He knew nothing about childbirth and had never attended childbirth classes. A nurse asked if he would come to the delivery room with his wife. But he shook his head: no. He was afraid—and besides, he believed that birth was women's business and that the delivery room was no place for fathers. Both Maria and the nurse tried to convince him otherwise, but Dominic still declined. The nurse shrugged her shoulders.

But when the time of birth was near, sensing how important it was to Maria to have her husband with her in the delivery room, the nurse asked Dominic, "Will you help wheel your wife down the corridor?" How could he refuse? He took one end of the bed and wheeled her away. Once he was in the delivery room, the door behind him swung shut. He looked around apprehensively and realized that he had been tricked. He would have left at that moment had his wife not screamed out during a powerful contraction. Instead, he took her hand.

Within a few minutes, the baby was born. Dominic looked at his newborn son like a man in love. When asked if he was glad he attended the birth, his emotion prevented him from answering. Tears streaming down his cheeks, he nodded his head firmly up and down.

As a father, you are not alone in your doubts. Most fathers feel this way. But you don't need to be an expert on labor to reduce the mother's fear and pain during labor and maximize her joy in giving birth. All you need to do is follow the simple instructions in this book. They will get you through labor smoothly from the first contraction until after the baby is born.

Fathers do have an important place in childbirth. If you are willing to be nurturing, to prepare for labor with your partner, and to read this book and follow the suggestions herein, you will be a highly effective childbirth companion. Many fathers want to be the primary and sole birth partner, but you may want to share labor support with another person—a relative, friend, or doula. The father alone can help the mother through labor, but he may prefer to give just emotional support and share the birth experience while another person gives practical, hands-on support. "I wanted to be an ever-present help during labor," said Dean, the father of a baby boy. "And I wanted to be at the birth. But my wife, Rya, and I hired a doula…to give the lion's share of support."

The father's presence is important even with a doula. Ideally, the doula is present to support both parents. She will maximize the father's involvement during childbearing as she helps the mother to better cope with labor. But no one can share what you can share as a father: your love. Anne, the mother of two children, stated, "I definitely would have wanted my husband, Stan, to be there with me. But it's taken me two labors to know that I need someone else as well. Stan was good at making sure our birth plans were met, such as making sure I didn't labor on my back. But contractions lost him. I don't think he had any concept of how much I needed to be told what to do, but just being there, he helped me a great deal. I would have felt very alone had he not been there."

As the father, you can be the ideal childbirth companion. After all, you know the mother best. You can best respond to her emotional needs and can thereby most easily reduce the fear and pain of labor. But you can't be overprepared for labor. Read this book through. Anne's advice is this: "Learn as much about labor as you can. Do as much reading as your partner does. Realize that different women cope with contractions differently. Some women don't need to be told how to cope but will still need encouragement and reassurance at various points in time, others will need suggestions to be given to them, others will need to be told exactly what to do while the contraction is happening, and some will need techniques such as back counterpressure to be used to relieve some of the pain. Still others will just need you by their side."

Whatever your background is regarding childbirth, bear in mind that you have something that no one else has: your special relationship with your partner. This will help you be a soothing presence to her. And the most effective support you can give is your love.

WHAT IF I DON'T HAVE TIME TO READ THE WHOLE BOOK?

If you don't have time to read this book before labor begins, or if you are picking up this book for the first time and labor has already begun, don't worry. You can still assist a woman through labor. You can still be her guide.

If you don't have time to read this book cover to cover before labor begins, just plunge right in with chapter 4. If labor is under way and contractions are more than 7 minutes apart, begin with chapter 5 and follow the instructions there. This book will lead you from the first labor contraction through the time after the baby is born. You will gain the insight you need to be an effective childbirth companion.

Chapter Two

· · · · · · · · · · ·

UNDERSTANDING LABOR

$\mathcal{U}$nderstanding labor is key to giving effective support. If you know what to expect during labor, you will be in a better position to assist the mother. This chapter discusses two essential things: how labor affects the mother's body and how labor affects her mind and behavior.

SIGNS THAT LABOR MIGHT BEGIN SOON

Premonitory signs usually, but not always, precede labor's onset. The mother may experience none, one, or all of the following signs:

Lightening and engagement. For first-time mothers, the baby's head usually drops lower into the pelvis 1–3 weeks before birth. The head is said to engage in the bony pelvis and is no longer movable. At the same time, the mother may experience lightening, which means that she carries the baby lower and has less pressure on the ribs and less shortness of breath. When lightening occurs, she may feel more awkward walking and have a more frequent need to urinate. "Lightening was a relief to me," recalled Tessa about her first pregnancy. "Finally I was able to breathe more easily and I had less pressure. However, I had to go to the bathroom all the time and I waddled like an inebriated duck." For mothers who have given birth before, engagement and lightening may not occur until labor actually begins.

An increase in Braxton-Hicks contractions. The mild uterine contractions that occur on and off throughout pregnancy, called Braxton-Hicks contractions, may occur more frequently and be more pronounced right before labor. "I knew labor was on the way," remarked Edna of the final weeks of her pregnancy. "Warm-up contractions were taking place much more frequently. I was hoping these practice contractions were doing their job effacing and dilating the cervix."

Bloody show. The mucus plug in the cervix, which seals off the uterus from infection, is discharged a day or two, or sometimes a week, before labor begins. Bloody show may appear as a pink glob of mucus, and it is often tinged with streaks of blood. The blood is from tiny capillaries in the cervix that rupture as the cervix softens and begins to open. The mother may or may not notice the release of this blood-tinged mucus. "I had a discharge of bloody show a couple of days before labor began," recalled Shahana. "There was a blob of blood-tinged mucus. I knew what this signified and I was very excited."

A decrease in fetal movements. The baby may become less active, as if he or she is storing up energy for the big day. "I noticed the baby didn't move as much," recalled Kat about the period before labor began. "At first I was worried. But I consulted my doctor, and she assured me that a decrease in the baby's movements was normal in advance of labor."

Diarrhea. Prelabor diarrhea sometimes, but not always, clears the bowels before labor begins. "Diarrhea the day before labor began seemed like nature's way of preparing for the birth process," recalled Jennifer, a new mother. "I had heard that women sometimes pass a little stool during second-stage labor. But it was already taken care of for me."

Rupture of membranes or bag of waters. In about 10–15 percent of mothers, the membranes rupture prior to labor, and there is a loss of water through the vagina. The water may flow out of the vagina in a trickle or a gush. Someone should inform the mother's health-care provider when membranes rupture. Moreover, the fluid should be clear. If it is dark or has a strong odor, the mother should consult her doctor or midwife without delay, as this may indicate possible fetal distress.

Some health-care providers insist that the mother begin labor within 24 hours of the rupture of membranes. If contractions do not begin spontaneously, health-care providers artificially induce labor to prevent infection. However, that intervention is seldom necessary. The mother can often safely wait for labor to begin naturally, provided that she avoids tub baths and sexual intercourse and inserts nothing into the vagina, including a tampon. She should also watch carefully for signs of infection.

In recalling the week before her labor began, Kat said: "My membranes ruptured and water exploded from me in a great gush. I was afraid of the cord preceding the baby's head, which can be fatal to the baby, and I checked with my midwife. She examined me and found everything to be just fine. She advised me to take my temperature twice every day and report to her immediately if I had an elevation in temperature. This way, if I had an infection, she would suggest inducing labor. But my temperature didn't rise. I went into labor normally a week or so after membranes had ruptured."

A spurt of energy. Frequently, a spurt of energy precedes labor's onset. "I had a great rush of energy before labor began," recalled Linda. "It was as if I were being given a dose of adrenaline to prepare myself for the birth."

Nesting instinct. The day before or several days before labor begins, the mother may feel a sudden urge to clean her home and prepare a place for the baby. Before our own third labor began, my wife, Jan, and I both spontaneously felt a need to get a place ready for the baby. We unpacked the stuff we had gotten ready for the great event—receiving blankets, baby clothes, and diapers—and we got the cradle ready. We were just in time for labor. Contractions began within 4 hours of the time we prepared a place for our child.

An intuition that labor will soon begin. The mother or father may sense that labor is imminent any time from a few hours to a few days before labor's onset. Eric recalls the dramatic moments of his partner's first labor. "I had a premonition that labor would begin within 2 days," he said. "It is difficult to put into words. It was just a sixth sense. It was all the more remarkable because Janet had none of the signs of premonitory labor. But my premonition was accurate. Contractions began on the second day."

TRUE LABOR OR FALSE LABOR

It is half past midnight. Laura awakens from a deep sleep with a sensation of invisible fingers tightening around her lower abdomen. Her first contraction! She is tremendously excited; her drowsiness vanishes. Fifteen minutes later, another contraction lasts about 30 seconds. She makes a mental list of everything she will bring to the hospital. Half an hour later, she feels another contraction.

The contractions are irregular. One lasts 30 seconds, and another 20. They are spaced at intervals of 15–40 minutes. Laura showers and dresses with a mixture of joyful expectancy and anxiety.

It has been 30 minutes since her last contraction. She goes into the kitchen, makes herself a cup of tea, and waits by the clock. Another 30 minutes goes by as she lingers over her tea. She still waits. Another half hour passes. There are no more contractions.

This is a description of one of the many ways a woman may

experience false labor—uterine contractions that feel like the real thing but peter out in time or with activity. Occasionally, a mother may feel what she thinks are labor contractions and tell her childbirth companion that the big moment has arrived, only to find out it is false labor.

False labor can occur any time after the thirtieth week of pregnancy (a full-term pregnancy lasts approximately 40 weeks). The following characteristics will help you distinguish the counterfeit from the real thing:

- True labor contractions dilate the cervix. False labor contractions do not dilate the cervix.
- True labor contractions occur at shorter and shorter intervals. False labor contractions usually occur at irregular intervals.
- True labor contractions gradually become stronger as time passes and labor progresses. False labor contractions do not become stronger as time passes.
- True labor contractions are usually intensified by walking. False labor contractions usually stop or slow down with a change of activity.
- True labor contractions are usually felt in the lower back and extend from the back to the front of the abdomen. False labor contractions are usually felt in the lower abdomen or groin.
- True labor contractions do not usually stop once they have started. False labor contractions usually peter out in time.

THE LABORING BODY

Every labor, like every snowflake, is unique. Labor may begin with a long period of mild contractions, as subtle as ripples on a still lake, or with intense contractions, more reminiscent of a storm at sea. Labor may progress continuously from beginning to end, or the uterus may rest midway, anywhere from a few minutes to several hours. There is a wide range of variation in normal labor. But all labors follow the stages here:

First stage. Contractions efface (thin) and dilate (open) the cervix. First-stage labor is divided into three additional stages of early or latent labor, active or late labor, and transition.

Second stage. The baby is born. The mother usually bears down (pushes) with contractions.

Third stage. Contractions cause the placenta (afterbirth) to be born.

The mother most needs your support during active labor and transition in the first stage and during second-stage labor.

LENGTH OF LABOR

The overall length of labor, as well as the lengths of individual stages and phases of labor, varies tremendously. One mother may labor and give birth in an hour and a half. Another mother may be in labor for 2 or 3 days. The labor of the mother you are supporting may be quite different from the averages described here, and that is perfectly normal. To be an effective childbirth companion, it is essential to be flexible and to respond to labor as it unfolds.

LABOR CONTRACTIONS

Labor consists of a series of contractions. During a contraction, the uterus rhythmically tightens and relaxes. Contractions come and go in waves and continue intermittently until the cervix is dilated and the baby and placenta are born. Each contraction builds in intensity, reaches a peak, and then tapers off, leaving a period of rest before the next contraction begins. At the peak of a contraction, the uterus, which you can feel through the mother's abdomen, becomes firm and hard to the touch.

CONTRACTIONS AND THE CERVIX

Contractions cause changes in the cervix. The cervix is the lowest portion of the uterus, which protrudes into the vagina. In Latin, *cervix* means "neck," and the cervix is sometimes referred to as the neck of the womb. You can feel the cervix with a finger deep inside the vagina. Before pregnancy and close to birth, it feels like a moist, rounded ball of muscle, like the tip of a nose. Hormones manufactured during pregnancy make the cervix as soft as lips by the time labor begins. During labor, it grows even softer, as soft as an earlobe. In that state, the cervix becomes amazingly stretchy, like the neck of a turtleneck sweater.

Effacement

Prior to the onset of labor, the cervix is said to be ripe—that is, softer, shorter, and sometimes partially open. During labor, the cervix, which is an inch or more thick, continues to thin and shorten. The thick, muscular cervix becomes paper thin and is taken up by the uterus. This process is called effacement.

Cervical effacement is measured in percentages. For first births, the cervix is usually 75–100 percent effaced before it begins to dilate (open). During second and subsequent births, the cervix often begins dilating before it has effaced that much.

For many mothers, the cervix is partially or fully effaced and dilated 1–2 centimeters before labor begins.

Dilation

Once labor begins, uterine contractions dilate the cervical opening, called the os, from the size of a dimple to a passage wide enough for the baby's head, about the size of a grapefruit. This process is known as dilation (or sometimes dilatation). The approximate dilation of the cervix is measured from 1–10 centimeters. When the cervix is dilated to 10 centimeters, it is said to be fully dilated. This is first-stage labor, which is determined by vaginal exam and dilation. The baby then journeys through a gateway to new life, from the uterus through the stretchy birth canal and into the parents' waiting arms.

Station

The distance the baby's head descends into the mother's pelvis, or station, is another sign of labor's progress and is also measured by vaginal exam. You will probably hear nurses or the mother's physician or midwife talking in terms of "degrees of station." This refers to the position of the baby's head in relation to two bony projections, the ischial spines, at the approximate midpoint of the mother's pelvis. Stations of –3, –2, and –1 indicate that the baby's head is that many centimeters above the ischial spines. Stations of 1, 2, and 3 indicate that the baby's head is that many centimeters below the ischial spines. When the head is engaged, or settled in the pelvis, it is at station 0. The head usually engages approximately 2 weeks before labor in first-time mothers and at the beginning of labor for mothers who have given birth before.

FIRST-STAGE LABOR

The cervix thins and opens during the long first stage of labor. Besides effacing and dilating the cervix, the powerful rhythmic contractions also prepare the baby for his or her first breath. As the uterine walls tighten and relax, they massage the baby, stimulate the circulatory system, and aid in the expulsion of mucus and fluid from the baby's lungs.

First-stage labor may last from 2 or 3 hours to 36 hours or longer, and the average length of the first stage is about 12 hours. Labor is usually, but not always, shorter for mothers who have given birth before.

First-stage contractions usually begin about 20–30 minutes apart and occur at shorter and shorter intervals until they come every 2–3 minutes. First-stage contractions usually last between 30 and 90 seconds each. At the beginning of labor, the contractions are usually short, and they become longer toward the end of labor. As labor progresses, the intensity of contractions increases from mild in early first-stage labor to intense during late first-stage labor.

The three phases of first-stage labor (early labor, late labor, and transition) are distinct but more or less blend into one another. Early labor contractions are generally mild, gentle, and easily managed. By the active labor phase, contractions become stronger. During transition, contractions are at their most intense.

Early Labor (Latent Phase)

In early labor, the cervix dilates to 3–5 centimeters. Contractions last from 30–45 seconds and occur at decreasing intervals with plenty of time to rest between each one, for example, from 20 minutes to 5 minutes.

The first contractions are usually similar to menstrual cramps, beginning in the back and girdling around to the front. The mother can usually continue her normal activities for several hours before labor demands most of her attention.

Marinda, the new mother of a boy, recounted this: "Labor began in the middle of the night like it does with so many mothers. My husband, Frank, told me to go back to sleep for a few hours. But I was excited! Telling me to go back to sleep was like telling a child to go to sleep on Christmas morning. I got up and did stuff around the house, all night long, and after a while Frank got up to be with me. I am glad I was awake to experience labor. It was very exciting!"

Lauren recalled her early labor this way: "I had a great time during early labor. My husband, Aaron, and my labor support person, Rita, sat in the living room and listened to music. We went through photograph albums for hours, just reminiscing and talking about how the baby's photos would fit in."

Some women skip the early labor phase. Our first labor had no early phase. It began with a cataclysmic burst of energy. There was no time to go back to sleep or continue ordinary activities. From the very first contraction, labor required all of Jan's concentration. Contractions came every 5 minutes and lasted 60–75 seconds. Jan was in late active labor from the very beginning.

Active Labor (Late Labor)

During active (late) labor, the cervix dilates from 3–5 centimeters to 7–8 centimeters. Contractions last from 45–75 seconds each and occur at decreasing intervals, such as from 7 minutes to 2 minutes (the average range being from 5 minutes to 3 minutes).

The contractions become much more intense and much more uncomfortable during this phase. The mother's need for labor support is greater as well. She will probably need your help through active labor to make labor more bearable.

Andrea went through active labor with her friend Peter, who

before attending childbirth classes, knew nothing about labor. She said, "We alternated walking around the birthing room together and me sitting in a rocking chair while Peter massaged my shoulders. Contractions were very hard at times but never more than I could bear. Just having Peter with me gave me strength and helped me cope."

Emily, a first-time mother who spent active labor with her friend Susie, had this to say: "Late labor was all encompassing for me. I didn't want to talk very much. I just wanted to be held and told that everything would be OK. Susie was fantastic. She held me close. She talked me through contractions, and she led me through guided imagery, which helped me cope immensely. I am glad I had her with me."

Transition

During the transition phase, the cervix dilates to 10 centimeters. Contractions last 60–120 seconds each and occur at variable intervals, ranging from 2–3 minutes.

Many women do not notice a distinct transition phase. For them, transition is just another part of active labor. For other mothers, transition is a distinct phase and is the most difficult part of labor.

The mother may perspire with her contractions. She may become nauseated and vomit. Some women have a premature urge to push during this phase. The need for continuous labor support is greatest during transition. The mother will probably need you during every minute. Your support will give her the strength to get through transition smoothly.

Emma, a new mother, said of transition, "I never imagined contractions could be so incredibly intense. I needed my husband, John, there right by my side every minute. I didn't even want him to leave to go to the bathroom. When he did have to leave for a minute or two, he made sure a nurse was at my side, talking me through contractions."

In a similar vein, Cara stated, "Transition was the most difficult part of labor for me. I leaned on my labor support person, Edna, every second. She helped me relax when tension in my body was causing me more pain. With her help, I surrendered to contractions and made it through this difficult part of labor."

SECOND STAGE (BIRTH)

The second stage may last from a few minutes to several hours, and the average length is 1–2 hours. The second stage is the most exciting part of labor because it is when the baby is born. The mother usually becomes actively involved with labor during this stage, bearing down (pushing) with contractions. Between contractions, she may fall into a dreamy half-waking, half-sleeping state.

With each new contraction, the baby's head moves slightly farther down the birth canal. Then, when the uterus relaxes between contractions, the head slips back up again. The baby's descent puts pressure on the rectum. The mother may feel as if she needs to move her bowels. This is usually a sign that birth is imminent. The mother may pass some feces as the baby descends. This is part of normal birth.

You may see the lips of the vagina begin to part as the baby continues his or her downward passage. Within a short while the baby's head (or buttocks if the baby is breech) will appear. If the baby is in the headfirst presentation, you may first glimpse the baby as a spot of moist, dark hair at the end of a fleshy tunnel.

Eventually, a portion of the head about the size of an grapefruit appears and no longer slips back at the end of each contraction. This is called crowning. With a few more contractions, the baby will be born.

The head is usually born with the face toward the mother's back; then it rotates to one side. The shoulders—first one, then the other—are born and the rest of the body follows quickly.

The baby is born wet from amniotic fluid and is usually covered with varying amounts of *vernix caseosa* (Latin for "cheesy varnish"), a white emollient substance that protects the baby in utero.

The curly bluish white umbilical cord stretches from the baby to the placenta, still inside the mother. Initially, the baby is usually bluish gray in color. The skin becomes more pink in a short while.

Your labor support—from helping the mother avoid tearing to sharing emotionally this dramatic stage of labor—is needed

throughout the second stage. You and the mother will probably be very excited during this part of labor.

Marie, a new mother, said, "Ron helped me throughout
the birth process. Each time I changed positions, he
assisted me and supported me in my position of choice. I
gave birth in a semi-squatting position with Ron standing
behind me, supporting me with his arms under my arms
holding me up."

Lee, another new mother, said, "My husband wanted
to catch the baby himself. He was so excited. He assisted
me during birth by helping me with a birth position and
massaging the area between the vagina and anus to keep
me from tearing. When we first saw the baby's head, a mere
walnut-sized part descending through the birth canal, he got
into position. I was laying on my side on the birthing bed
and he was kneeling at my feet. When the baby came, my
doctor assisted with the first part of the birth of the head.
Then my husband put his hands into place and 'caught' the
baby. He handed me my newborn child almost immediately
and I began breast-feeding. It was wonderful!"

THIRD STAGE

The third stage of labor occurs shortly after birth and usually takes
only a few minutes. In this stage, contractions are usually mild.

Also, the placenta, sometimes called afterbirth, is delivered.
Throughout pregnancy, this amazing organ is responsible for

the transfer of food and oxygen from the mother's bloodstream to the baby via the umbilical cord. The mother usually bears down with one or two contractions and the placenta usually slips out easily. The placenta is shaped like a disc. The side attached to the uterus is red and meaty; the other side, to which the umbilical cord is attached, is covered with shiny membranes. The physician or midwife briefly examines the placenta to be sure it is intact. Occasionally, a piece remains in the uterus and must be removed. When the placenta is delivered, the mother might discharge quite a bit of blood. This is normal.

Breast-feeding immediately after the baby is born assists in the delivery of the placenta and the conclusion of labor. When the baby sucks on the nipples, the mother's pituitary gland in the brain releases the hormone oxytocin, which causes the uterus to contract and deliver the placenta.

After the placenta is delivered, breast-feeding helps prevent postpartum hemorrhage. The release of oxytocin helps keep the uterine muscles clamped tightly around the open blood vessels at the placental site.

THE PAIN OF LABOR

Labor is painful at times for most mothers. The degree of pain varies widely from woman to woman. One mother may find labor quite painful and difficult while another finds labor less difficult or, rarely, not at all painful.

Various factors influence the degree of the mother's

discomfort. These include the size and position of the baby; the shape of the mother's pelvis; the mother's degree of relaxation or tension; her thoughts and feelings about birth; whether or not she feels comfortable, secure, and at peace in the birthing environment; and above all, the quality of labor support she receives.

Contractions occurring during transition are usually the most painful ones. The second stage for many mothers is usually, but not always, less painful; for others it is just as difficult as the first stage; but for some others it is even enjoyable.

The childbirth companion may fear that he or she will have a difficult time supporting the mother when she is pain. Many expectant fathers, in particular, are reluctant to see their partner or spouse in pain. Bear in mind, however, that your support can greatly reduce the mother's discomfort and make her labor progress more smoothly. Don't expect to be able to eliminate all the pain of labor. Nothing can do this—short of powerful drugs that interfere with both labor and the baby's health. You can reduce much of her pain as effectively as most drugs can.

The unique pain of labor is often referred to as positive pain. It is healthy pain. Each contraction is purposeful, opening the cervix during the first stage and birthing the baby during the second stage. Above all, bear in mind that labor, unlike other painful experiences, encompasses a wide variety of feelings, from discomfort to ecstasy. And though labor is often painful at times, many women describe it as a rich, rewarding experience, and no one would say that of a toothache.

"I am a coward about pain," says Eleanor, one mother of two children. "But labor's pain was different. I felt able to experience it without too much fear. It wasn't like any other pain I had ever experienced. I can honestly say I enjoyed labor both times. I doubt if I would be able to say that if it weren't for my husband, Jonathan. He helped me relax and let go and flow with labor's contractions. I think that was the key between a painful and an enjoyable experience: my ability to flow with contractions."

THE LABORING MIND RESPONSE

When it comes to giving labor support, insight into the mother's psychological changes and unique behavior is even more important than knowing about the physical changes of labor. After all, the childbirth companion does not see the cervix dilate. However, he or she does see the mother's altered behavior and experiences her altered state of mind. Understanding what happens in the laboring mother's mind—as described in this section—is the foundation for giving effective labor support.

Understanding the psycho-emotional dimensions of labor is especially important because labor, like love making, is an emotionally sensitive process. Emotions and thoughts influence labor. What the mother thinks and feels influence her contractions, including how much pain she feels, and the length of her labor. Her ability to let go and flow with the altered state of being that labor ushers in is directly proportionally to her enjoyment of childbearing.

If you understand the laboring mother's altered state of mind and behavior, you will be better able to give support tailored to her needs. By meeting her needs, you will positively influence her labor, make her feel more comfortable, and help her surrender to the force that will bring her child into the world.

During early labor, the mother may be like her usual self. She may react with a mixture of anxiety and excitement. She may be quite talkative. But as early labor merges into the active phase, profound psychological changes occur. As Aidan, one new father, put it: "It was as if she were in a different world, traveling in a new dimension as she lay in my arms." Passionate emotions are released. The laboring mother becomes a more primal, instinctive being; it is as if the contractions that open the cervix also open the door on an instinctive part of the self.

The laboring woman experiences any of seven things that, taken together, make up what I call the laboring mind response— a natural psycho-physiological reaction to the labor process.

First, as labor progresses, the mother experiences an altered state of consciousness. She enters a more primal, instinctive state of mind. She becomes less rational and more intuitive. Her concentration narrows. She focuses inward. She is wholly caught up in the force that will birth her child. Her contractions and her childbirth companion become her world. The mother may forget what she has learned in childbirth classes or through reading about how to cope with labor, and she may depend on her birth partner to remind her.

As the new father Robin explained, "Gone was all we learned in childbirth classes. Gone was all we practiced. The relaxation exercises, the breathing patterns, meant nothing. Suddenly, Maria was a new being under the sun. She had forgotten everything we learned together! Luckily, I learned along with her and I reminded her what to do when contractions mounted in intensity. I was surprised how well she responded to me. It was as if I were the only one in the world at that time."

Second, while the mother is becoming more instinctive, she becomes more "right brained." As labor progresses, the mother's energy shifts from the left hemisphere, associated with logical, mathematical thought, to the right hemisphere, which is associated more with artistic thought and creativity. She ceases to be analytical. If she lets go, she is likely to flow with labor. Surrender is key. The childbirth companion can help the mother surrender to the power that will bring her child from the uterus to her waiting arms. The more the mother is able to flow with her state of mind, the more likely it is that she will have a smooth labor.

One of the main reasons guided imagery (see chapter 3) is such an effective labor coping tool is that guided imagery is right-brain oriented and seems tailor made to the laboring mother's right-hemisphere orientation. Guided imagery gives her positive images and thoughts in the language of the right hemisphere. For example, instead of picturing the cervix dilating, she can imagine an opening flower. The right hemisphere makes the connection between the opening flower and the dilating cervix.

As labor progresses, the third step is that the mother's perceptions of, for example, space and time, become altered or distorted. Contractions may seem to go on for longer than they actually are and to be endless. The childbirth companion can help the mother gain perspective by giving continuous support and helping her through one contraction at time.

Serena, the new mother of a baby girl, recalled: "I thought contractions were going on forever. There seemed to be no end to labor. I depended on Jim to get me through labor. He calmly kept me taking it one contraction at a time until I was in second stage and beside myself with joy."

Fourth, during labor, the mother experiences heightened emotional sensitivity and vulnerability. She becomes utterly dependent on her childbirth companion and those surrounding her. This is one reason the childbirth companion's nurturing presence is so vital.

As stated earlier, emotions influence labor. The laboring mother is highly emotional, and her emotions influence her contractions and how long labor will last. Because of this, developing a positive birth plan is essential to experiencing a normal labor. The mother should choose a birthing environment in which she feels at peace and able to let go emotionally. She should choose a physician or midwife whom she likes and whom she feels comfortable with while experiencing her deepest emotions.

"I never realized how much emotions influenced labor until I was actually in labor," said Amy. "I am fortunate in that I planned my birth so that I would be at peace during labor. Ron, my husband, was emotionally supportive. He helped me feel nurtured. This made a big difference in my experience of labor."

Fifth, the laboring woman exhibits distinctly sexual behavior. The laboring woman often looks and sounds like a woman nearing sexual climax. She may moan and sigh and groan and be unconcerned with who sees her unclothed body. She becomes intensely emotional and near the time of birth may wear a tortured ecstatic expression like a woman on the edge of orgasm.

Sixth, the laboring mother may experience lowered inhibitions. The mother may lose all of her social inhibitions. She may not care about the opinions of those around her. Many laboring women remove all their clothing. This is particularly common during home or childbearing-center births, where the atmosphere is conducive to a spontaneous response to labor.

Jack, a new father who helped his partner through labor, recalled, "I knew labor was under way for real when Diana took off her clothes. It wasn't necessary to be undressed to see anything going on. She just did it automatically. I am glad I learned that this was a natural part of labor."

It is essential to realize that decreased inhibitions are a normal reaction to labor. Don't interfere with the mother's lowered inhibitions or the actions they generate. Rather, welcome this as a sign that labor is progressing just the way it should.

Seventh, the mother experiences increased openness to suggestion. In her vulnerable state of mind, the laboring mother is highly sensitive to the actions and words of those around her, as well as to her own thoughts, feelings, and views toward birth. This is one reason developing a positive attitude is so important. The critical remarks of others or tension and disturbances in the birthing environment all affect the laboring mother deeply, and by so doing, they also affect the physiology of labor, often causing longer, more difficult contractions. By the same token, the positive words and thoughts of a childbirth companion can bring about a smoother, more efficient labor for the mother. For example, the coping tool of guided imagery may be more effective than patterned breathing as a coping tool during labor because guided imagery uses suggestion. Coached in the language of the right hemisphere, guided imagery gives the mother positive suggestions at a time when she is most open to suggestion.

THE SEXUALITY OF CHILDBIRTH

Closely allied to the laboring mind response is the fact that childbirth is a sexual process. Appreciating the sexuality of childbirth goes a long way toward enabling the childbirth companion to give support appropriate to the mother's state of body and mind. The childbirth companion who accepts this aspect of labor will understand why it is so important to be a nurturing presence. The most important kind of support you can give is your love.

At first sight, love making and labor are poles apart. Love making is associated with pleasure and labor is associated with pain. But labor is a sexual process in that it takes place within the sexual organs. Striking similarities exist between sex and labor. During both labor and sex:

- The uterus rhythmically contracts (though the contractions are far more intense during labor).
- The hormone oxytocin is released.
- The right brain is engaged.
- The woman becomes intensely emotional.
- Emotions influence the process.
- Social inhibitions decrease.
- The woman may sigh, moan, and groan.
- The woman's facial expression may become ecstatic.
- Disturbances in the room can impair the process.
- A state of well-being frequently follows.

When you make comparisons between sex and labor, it becomes clearer why radiating a positive attitude toward birth is so vital to the mother's experience of labor. Our attitudes affect labor just as they affect love making.

Peter, a new father who was instrumental in helping his partner, Cindy, through labor, had this to say: "I think that the comparisons between love making and labor were the most important thing I learned about my support-giving role. This wasn't covered during our childbirth classes, which meant the classes were worse than nothing because they pretend to educate you. I had to learn about the sexuality of childbirth by reading. When I discovered this facet of childbearing, I suddenly understood why being nurturing to my mate, Cindy, was more important than a hundred breathing patterns. The fact that I was able to be nurturing was what got her through labor in the terrible environment of a high-risk medical center."

The same conditions that support satisfying love making are conducive to efficient labor: a peaceful atmosphere, the presence of a loved one, and emphasis on positive emotions. By the same token, the same conditions that impair love making, including a disturbance in the environment and negative emotions, can impede labor's progress. Understanding this aspect of labor is essential in making good birth plans and in giving effective labor support.

Love making and labor are both more satisfying when the woman sets aside the analytical mind and surrenders to the process. By being a nurturing presence, showing her that you care, and giving her positive suggestions, you can enable the mother to do just that.

Chapter Three

· · · · · · · · · · ·

PREPARING FOR LABOR

lthough the childbirth companion can help the mother through labor without making any advance preparations whatsoever, there is no substitute for being well prepared. The well-prepared birth partner will know how to help the laboring woman relax during difficult contractions, how to relieve her back pain, how to calm her if she is panicking, how to prevent her from tearing, and a host of other things.

"I am glad Roger learned about labor," said Linda about the birth of her two children. "I doubt he could have helped out during labor to the same phenomenal degree that he did if he wasn't prepared for the big event. He knew precisely how to help me when I had back pain, how to support me when I felt I was losing it during contractions, and how to keep me from tearing as my babies were born."

"Learn all you can about childbirth," advises Rick, the father of two boys. "There is no substitute for learning about labor.

You will be more secure in your supportive role if you read about childbirth and educate yourself about birth."

Amy, the mother of a baby girl, says, "I can't recommend it too strongly: Get familiar with your role in childbirth. Meet the hospital staff if you are giving birth in a hospital. Attend prenatal exams. Read what your mate reads. Practice support-giving techniques such as back counterpressure. You will be more secure in your role during labor and better able to support your partner." This advice goes for family and friends as well as for fathers. Be prepared for labor. The father should attend childbirth classes if the couple opts for classes. Family members or friends will also benefit from attending classes. If you cannot attend all the classes, try to attend one or two.

If the mother doesn't attend childbirth classes, you can still prepare for labor by reading what the mother reads, viewing a childbirth film, and practicing supportive methods like relaxation. To view a childbirth film, contact a local childbirth educator and ask whether you can sit in at the next showing of a birth film. Chances are that the educator will be glad to have you. Phillip, a new father, recalled: "Although we were planning a hospital birth, we audited a birth film in a home-birth class because it gave a more realistic description of labor and a woman's reaction to labor. It depicted the mother groaning and moaning and making sensual sounds. The hospital birth classes showed a woman all draped, which we were definitely not interested in. I recommend both the mother and father view a home birth film wherever they are planning to labor."

By preparing for labor, you will feel far more confident in your own role. As the new father Frank put it, "Everything went smoothly. There were no surprises because we practiced relaxation and massage, attended childbirth classes and visited the hospital together. We felt like we had gone though the dress rehearsal and this was the real thing."

Andrea, who attended her friend Rosalie's birth, had this to say: "Every labor is different and my own birth didn't fully prepare me to help Rosalie during labor. Only prenatal education prepared me. I didn't attend childbirth classes with Rosalie, but I read about labor. I was nervous, but I knew what to expect through the phases and stages of labor, especially the way a laboring woman behaves. It turns out that I helped Rosalie and her partner, Eric, more than I ever imagined I could."

To prepare for labor fully, develop a positive view toward birth; get familiar with the mother's birth plans; attend one, two, or more prenatal appointments; practice relaxation together; and practice guided imagery together.

ESSENTIALS OF A POSITIVE VIEW OF BIRTH

One of the most important things the childbirth companion can do in advance of labor is develop a positive view of birth. As mentioned in chapter 2, the mother becomes extremely sensitive and open to suggestion as her labor progresses. Your view of birth will affect the mother's labor. The childbirth companion's beliefs and attitudes about birth may be transmitted to the mother by even the subtlest words and actions and can actually affect labor's progress. If the birth partner has a positive image of birth, he or she will most likely be able to inspire the mother's confidence and help her cope effectively with labor.

A childbirth companion with a negative view of birth will impede the mother's ability to handle contractions normally. Unfortunately, many health-care professionals, including some obstetricians and even some midwives, have a negative or overly medical view of birth. They are educated about labor's complications but are not familiar with helping a mother give birth without complications. This is why it is so important to meet and interview your health-care provider before making a final decision about a whether that person will attend your birth.

Examine your own view of birth. How do you feel about labor? Do you believe that it is a healthy, natural function or a process to be endured? Do you believe the mother is strong and capable and that she gives birth, or do you believe that she is at the mercy of the hospital and staff? Many well-intentioned people picture labor as taking place in an impersonal hospital setting with the mother wearing a hospital gown, having intravenous feeding, and giving birth flat on her back with legs in stirrups while masked attendants mill about. Such a "medical" situation can be uncomfortable—especially when they draw a curtain between the mother and the wonderfully amazing experience of childbirth.

A positive view of birth does not mean that you believe labor is painless. It means that you believe that the mother is able to take contractions in stride and that, though labor is painful at times, it is a rewarding experience. Having a positive image of birth does not mean that you are expected to radiate confidence every minute you are with the mother during labor. This is unrealistic. You are bound to be afraid and nervous at times. Having a positive image means that you believe that childbirth is a joyful event and that you embody the following five elements.

Birth Is a Normal Process, Not an Illness

Labor is a normal physiological process, not an illness, but many well-intentioned people act as if it were. Karen recalled, "My labor support person was always looking for something to go wrong. It wasn't anything obvious in what she did; it was just a general attitude. It made me nervous and made it hard for me to handle contractions. I began to feel something would go wrong. And I knew if I kept thinking this way, something really would go wrong."

You will be better able to support the mother if, at the root of your attitudes, is the feeling that childbearing is normal. "I felt good about labor," expressed Ashley, a new mother. "I needed a birth companion who also felt positive about childbirth. My labor support person, Emily, believed that birth was a normal function like conception. Her basic attitude about labor was conveyed in her presence and in the support she gave."

Birth Is a Natural Process, Not a Medical Event

Because the majority of labors today take place in the hospital, which we associate with medical procedures and illness, we come to think almost automatically of birth as a medical process. For many childbirth companions, it takes an effort to view birth as the natural event it is. "Birth ought to take place in the home," said Stephanie, a new mother of a baby boy who was born at home. "There is nothing dangerous about giving birth that requires hospitalization unless the mother is really sick. If the parents are unwilling to give birth at home, they should select a hospital with a homelike setting. And more important than the setting are the attitudes of the staff. Do they treat labor as a natural process, or do they approach it like a medical procedure? All the support in the world can't make up for a staff with a negative view of birth."

By reminding yourself that childbirth is a natural event, you will be less likely to panic at the first sign of pain. You will take labor in stride. Wherever the mother plans to give birth—home, a childbearing center, or the hospital—get rid of the view that the laboring woman is an invalid, and replace it with images of health and beauty. After all, the laboring woman is radiantly healthy; she is at the height of her creative power.

Believing that birth is a natural process does not mean that a woman is committed to giving birth without pain medication, though this is safest for mother and baby. Rather, it implies that the mother believes that birth is not a medical event but a physiologically natural process like conception.

Birth Is a Social Event

The birth of a child is the beginning of a family, and as such, it is the most significant social event in the lives of most couples. If couples focus on this aspect of birth rather than on medical procedures, labor will progress more smoothly. Focusing on the social event of birth will help the mother make birth plans appropriate to her experience. For instance, she will see herself as inviting her health-care provider to share this intimate event and choose a physician or midwife accordingly. Keeping the social aspect of birth in mind will enable the childbirth companion to see labor as a rite of passage into a new realm of being and not a medical procedure. As labor ushers the mother and father into parenthood, this dramatic rite initiates the baby into life outside the womb.

Childbirth should be just as special as a wedding. Of course, the two situations of childbirth and a wedding are completely different. However, both are life-altering social events for most couples. Viewing birth in the same light as you would view your wedding helps you make plans conducive to a physiologically normal birth. If a couple plans the birth as carefully as they plan their wedding, they will avoid much disappointment.

The Mother Is the Center of the Childbearing Drama

It is the mother's birth, the couple's baby, and the couple's strength and power that will bring the baby into the world.

I am often amazed to hear women say, "The hospital allowed my husband to be present throughout," or "The doctor allowed me to touch my baby as he was being born." I feel like saying, "It is your birth, your baby. Of course you have the right to do what you want to. The health-care provider and the hospital staff are present to serve you!" You invite the health-care provider to attend your birth and you pay his or her fee. You are in charge. Don't lose sight of this. If you want to have a positive birth experience, it is essential to select a health-care provider and hospital whose staff believes in these basic facts.

The Mother Is Responsible for Making Wise Choices

Making wise choices goes hand in hand with seeing oneself as the center of the childbearing drama. Because there are often so many options close to home, expecting parents must pay careful attention when exploring options and making sensible choices. This is up to the mother and the father. But as a childbirth companion with a positive image of birth, you may be able to influence the mother to take responsibility for making wise birth plans.

Too many people don't make concrete birth plans and then wonder why they are so bitterly disappointed after birth. It is up to the mother and her partner to make good choices.

This means the mother must select her birthing environment carefully and invite those she thinks will genuinely help her through labor.

THE BIRTH PLAN

One of the childbirth companion's main responsibilities is helping the mother achieve her individual goals for a safe, positive birth. To do this, the childbirth companion has to know what is most important to the mother besides, of course, a healthy baby. Get acquainted with the mother's feelings about intravenous feeding, electronic fetal monitoring, other medical procedures, use of pain-relief medication, artificial rupture of membranes, episiotomy (a surgical incision to enlarge the birth outlet as the baby is born), birthing position, breast-feeding, and length of postpartum stay.

You don't have to be an expert on any of these subjects, but you should know the mother's wishes. This allows you to better tailor your support to her individual needs. For example, Marissa, a mother who planned her birth carefully, recalled, "My labor support person was an immense help in making sure my birth plans were safeguarded. I wanted to labor without interference from analgesia and intravenous feeding. She was able to explain my position to the staff that I preferred to avoid medical intervention unless there was a genuine emergency."

The father should draw up birth plans with his partner, too.

Take time with your birth plans. Make a written birth plan if that helps you focus. Clarice, a new mother, said, "Jim and I made a thorough birth plan—not long enough to intimidate our health-care providers and hospital staff and make them think we were too demanding but long enough to cover all my needs. One thing that was very important to me was to remain with my baby for the first hours after birth without interruption. I had everyone sign this aspect of my birth plan to call attention to it. My written birth plan helped Jim and me focus on what I wanted during labor and helped the staff stay focused on what we really wanted to get out of the experience besides a live, healthy baby!"

Be sure to share your birth plans with your physician or midwife so that he or she can tailor care to your individual needs. "We made a written birth plan," said Angela about the birth of her first child. "We wanted to be sure my midwife knew what was important to me. For example, I wanted to labor without medication and I didn't want her suggesting medication at the last moment when I would be vulnerable and hard put to refuse. I also wanted my husband Derek with me at all times, during exams as well as other times, and we made that desire clear in my birth plan."

If your health-care provider does not agree with an important element in your birth plan, don't hesitate to change providers. Angela, who changed health-care providers during her third trimester, recalled, "It was very important for me to give birth without an episiotomy. This is unnecessary surgery. My doctor was reluctant to go along with me. He said he cuts episiotomies in nearly 100 percent of first-time mothers. So I switched doctors and never regretted the change. I gave birth with an intact perineum, something I would not have been able to do with my former doctor."

If you want to give birth without medication, it is important to select a health-care provider who is used to helping women labor naturally. If not, you are opening yourself up to making a difficult decision during labor. A doctor or nurse may suggest medication during your labor when you are least able to resist it.

You may decide to change your birth plans as pregnancy progresses and you learn more about labor and your options. You may add things or change your mind entirely about other elements in your birth plan. This is natural. Most women don't know a whole lot about labor when they first get pregnant. They learn about labor as time goes on and they read, attend classes, or hear about others' experiences in childbirth. Keep your health-care provider and the hospital staff updated with any changes in your birth plan.

ATTENDING PRENATAL APPOINTMENTS

Attend prenatal appointments with the woman you are planning to help through labor. The father should attend all prenatal appointments if at all possible. Other childbirth companions should attend one or two prenatal appointments. If the health-care provider has available hours only when you work, you will find it well worth your while to take off a short amount of time to be at the prenatal exam at least once or twice.

"Karen attended a couple of prenatal appointments with me," recalled Andrea, the mother of two children. "I felt she was really my childbirth companion when she was present during prenatal exams. She made me feel secure and comfortable by being there with me."

The father and his partner should choose the health-care provider and attend the first prenatal appointment together. Chose someone you both like and feel you can get along with. Of course, you want someone who is medically competent, but you also want someone you like, who answers your questions fully, and who is committed to helping you with your birth plans. Remember that childbirth is a social event: you are inviting this person to share one of your most intimate events. You don't want anyone present that you do not fully get along with.

You may not have solidified your birth plans when you first meet your physician or midwife. Ideally, you should see a health-care provider in early pregnancy. At that time, you may not know enough about labor and your medical options during childbearing to make a wise choice of health-care provider. Evaluate your physician or midwife in light of any new knowledge you gain. Don't hesitate to change health-care providers.

For example, some mothers decide in advance that they want to have epidural anesthesia. They fear they won't be able to stand the pain. However, when they learn that emotional support during labor can reduce pain, they often change their minds and opt for natural birth. In this case, it is best to select a health-care provider who is accustomed to helping mothers birth naturally. "I was sure I wanted an epidural," said Nikki on the birth of her first child. "I can't stand pain of any description, and I knew I would buckle during labor. But my husband, Bob, really had a dream about going natural. So I tried it. Bob was immensely helpful to me during labor. He had a really positive attitude toward birth and didn't hesitate to put his arms around me when I was stressed. The most important thing he did was tell me he loved me. That's what got me through labor. I was really surprised. I didn't feel much pain during labor. I think it is because Bob was so supportive."

Some women live in an area where they may not get their first choice for a health-care provider. In many clinics and community health centers, midwives and physicians rotate and attend births for a certain number of hours each day. Which physician or midwife will assist the expectant mother depends on who is on call that day. Under such circumstances, a mother and her childbirth companions may not be able to meet the birth attendant in advance of labor. The best way to cope with this situation is to have a written birth plan. You can discuss your wishes with the health-care provider you meet so that, if possible, your plans can go into your hospital chart before your due date. In this situation, the childbirth companion acts as consumer advocate in the hospital. Amanda, the new mother of a baby girl, explained, "I went to a group practice and never know who I'd get. My childbirth companion memorized all the essentials of my birth plans including how I felt about circumcision. That way she was able to be sure I got what I wanted during labor and the first hour or so after birth."

Whether or not you can meet the physician or midwife, there are several benefits of attending prenatal appointments:

· You will be familiar with the health-care provider who will be attending labor.
· You will be able to help the mother relax.
· You will be able to help the mother focus on the fact that birth is a normal event, not an illness.
· You will be able to ask questions.
· You will be able to air your concerns.

MASTERING RELAXATION

Relaxation is key to a smooth labor. The British obstetrician Grantly Dick-Read, a pioneer in natural childbirth and the author of the inspiring book *Childbirth without Fear*, has called attention to what he names the fear-tension-pain cycle. A contraction begins. The mother becomes afraid. She tenses up.

Her contractions become painful. She becomes more afraid, tenser, and the cycle spirals. However, if she is relaxed, she will labor with less pain.

It is natural to have some fear about childbirth. No matter how much the mother and her childbirth companion read and view films about childbirth, they really don't know what the labor will be like until the time comes. But being well informed can eliminate much unnecessary fear, and practicing relaxation techniques can almost entirely eliminate any tension.

Most childbirth classes teach a form of relaxation. In this book, we'll focus on forms of relaxation that are ideally suited to the pregnant and laboring woman. During pregnancy and labor, the mother is more open to suggestion than at other times. Many forms of relaxation use suggestion to help the mother completely relax body and mind.

Autogenic Stress Release

In this exercise, the mother makes mental "contact" with various parts of her body and is given relaxing suggestions as she continues to breathe rhythmically. She can practice autogenic stress release during pregnancy and then during labor. It will be easier for the mother to relax to suggestion and to your touch. Here are the steps the mother can follow:

· To begin, get into a comfortable position. Many women who are in late pregnancy prefer lying on their side to any other position. You can lie on your side with a pillow supporting your head and, if you want, a pillow between your knees.

· Dim the lights.

· Be sure that the telephone ringing or something else won't distract you.

· Close your eyes.

· Take a few deep breaths in through the nose, exhaling through slightly parted lips. Observe your breathing for a minute or two.

· Now, let your breathing become a little deeper, a little slower, without straining in any way.

· Continue to breathe in this slow, relaxing way throughout the exercise.

· With each breath in and each breath out, mentally repeat the following: My right arm is heavy and warm.

· After a half a minute or so, direct your attention to your left arm.

· Now, with each breath in and each breath out, say (mentally): My left arm is heavy and warm.

· Then do the same for the right and left leg, and then say: My uterus and pelvic organs are warm, comfortable, and relaxed.

· Observe your breathing, calm and regular.

· With the next breath out, say: It breathes me…It breathes me.

· Now say: The muscles of my back and neck are warm and relaxed.

· After a half a minute or so, with the next breath out, say: My jaw muscles are loose and relaxed.

· Now, with the next breath out, say: My forehead is cool.

· Now, with the next breath out, say: My eyelids are heavy and relaxed.

· Enjoy the sensation of complete relaxation for a minute or so.

· Tell yourself: "Because I can relax, I can labor and give birth better."

· When you are ready, take a deep breath, stretch gently, and open your eyes.

Touch Relaxation

In this form of relaxation, the mother will learn to release tension at her childbirth companion's touch. Practice touch relaxation a few times during pregnancy so that the mother can relax easily with this method during labor.

The woman should get into a comfortable position and then make a fist and tighten the muscles of one arm. The childbirth companion should place his or her hands around the tense arm and say, "Relax to my touch." Then the mother should try to relax to her childbirth companion's touch.

You can try this with the feet and legs, with the back, and forehead. Each time, the childbirth companion places his or her hands on the tense part of the body and says, "Relax to my touch."

Practicing Massage

You can learn some simple massage strokes in advance of labor to significantly reduce the mother's comfort and assist her in relaxing.

Back Counterpressure

Applying firm counterpressure to the lower back can do wonders for back pain during labor. Back pain, sometimes referred to as back labor, can be extremely uncomfortable. It may even persist between contractions and prevent the mother from relaxing. Such back pain, present in about one-quarter of labors, is often the result of the baby being in a posterior position, which means that the baby's skull rather than face rests against the mother's spine.

Practice giving back counterpressure once or twice to get the idea. Place one hand on the mother's hip to stabilize her. With the heel of your other hand, press firmly against the spine. You can rotate the heel in very small circles so the flesh of her back moves over the bone. Some women prefer pressure on the small of the back rather than directly on the spine.

During labor, ask the mother to tell you where to press and how much pressure to apply. You will find that as labor progresses, the place where you should apply counterpressure moves lower and lower on the back. Don't be surprised if the mother wants a great deal of pressure.

Inner-Thigh Massage

Some women find inner-thigh massage comforting and relaxing during late-first-stage labor. Practicing it once or twice will give you enough familiarity with it so you can do it during labor.

Curve your hands over one or both of the mother's legs and stroke firmly from the groin to the knees. Use slightly less pressure when you go back again from the knees to the groin. Use long, even strokes.

Effleurage

Effleurage is light fingertip massage in which you simply draw circles on the abdomen or upper thighs. Some women find effleurage on the abdomen and the inner thighs comforting during contractions.

You can do effleurage or the mother may prefer to do it herself in time to her breathing. Stand or sit near the mother, or sit behind her with your legs apart and her back leaning against your chest and your arms around the abdomen.

With one or both hands or the fingertips—whichever the mother prefers—draw small circles over the abdomen occasionally sweeping down over the inner thighs.

Keep the pressure light, as if you were stroking the baby's head.

Perineal Massage

Some childbirth professionals swear that perineal massage, begun during the middle of the third trimester, reduces the chance of tearing by stretching the tissue. It also makes the mother more aware of her pelvic floor region.

The mother can do perineal massage herself or you can do it for her. If the mother has vaginitis or herpes, don't do this exercise without first consulting her health-care provider.

To begin, first be sure your hands are clean. Use a lubricant such as K-Y Jelly if necessary. Insert one finger knuckle deep into the vagina. Make smooth semicircles, pressing downward gently and firmly but not to the point of discomfort. When it is comfortable for the mother, massage with two or three fingers. Continue for 2–3 minutes daily.

Practicing Breathing Patterns

A bewildering array of breathing patterns are taught in childbirth classes. Unfortunately, none of them really help the mother relax or reduce the pain of labor. At most, they are methods of distraction.

The mother may find that she wants to take a cleansing breath at the beginning and end of each contraction. This signals to those present that she is having a contraction and for her to relax. The mother should take a deep, audible breath in through the nose and let it out either through the nose or through slightly parted lips, whichever she prefers.

It is best to continue with deep, relaxing abdominal breathing throughout labor. To do deep abdominal breathing, the mother should breathe in either through the nose or through slightly parted lips, whichever she prefers. The abdomen should rise on the in-breath and lower as she breathes out.

Mary Ann, a mother who practiced breathing patterns in advance of labor, said: "I learned deep breathing, light chest breathing, and pant blowing in my childbirth classes. When labor was intense, the breathing didn't help me at all. My labor support person suggested I breathe rhythmically and deeply. That helped me most through the late part of labor."

Using Guided Imagery

Guided imagery is a means of translating positive thoughts into dynamic mental images. It is an especially effective method of preparing for childbirth and coping with labor. Guided imagery can reduce the mother's fear and pain, and even the length of labor. It is especially effective during labor because it is a right-brain process, and the laboring mother is oriented toward the right brain (see chapter 2). As mentioned earlier, during labor, the mother is very open to suggestion and will benefit from the positive suggestions of guided imagery. Guided imagery can be far more effective than patterned breathing.

Guided imagery may not seem that effective when you think about it before labor begins. But during labor, the mother enters a unique state of mind that makes guided imagery more effective. Emma, the mother of a baby boy, explained: "I didn't really trust the guided imagery. I felt I needed more structure to get me through labor. But I am glad I practiced it during pregnancy because I remembered what I had learned when the going got rough. And that's what got me through labor."

This section includes two exercises that most women find highly effective during contractions: "the special place" and "the radiant breath." Additional guided imagery exercises are in my book *Mind over Labor.*

When guiding the mother with imagery exercises, use a soft, gentle voice; pause after each step; and give the mother ample time to complete each step before going on to the next one. Don't think twice about being repetitive. The mother, who is following the steps, will not become bored, especially during labor. You can use the same or similar exercises with each contraction as long as the mother finds them helpful.

You can practice guided imagery, and the exercises that follow, during pregnancy. But you can also help the mother with guided imagery even if she hasn't practiced during pregnancy, although the exercise you use will be somewhat different. Helping her with guided imagery during labor if she has not practiced during pregnancy is included in chapter 5, "Helping Her Every Step of the Way: Active Labor."

The Special Place

In this exercise, the expectant mother creates her own "special place"—a personal sanctuary, a place of peace, comfort, security, and relaxation. With 2 or 3 weeks of regular practice, the mother will automatically associate her special place with relaxation, peace, comfort, and security. The expectant mother can then use this exercise as a way to relax body and mind—during pregnancy and later during labor. In addition to bringing about peace and relaxation, recalling the special place during labor will help the mother draw on inner reserves of strength and reduce pain during labor.

As Isabelle, mother of a baby girl, recalled: "I practiced my special place during pregnancy. During labor, Andy, my husband, reminded me of the images in my special place. I found it particularly helpful during early labor when I was making the transition from home to hospital. The hospital atmosphere was not so intimidating when I imagined myself in my special place. I also found the imagery very helpful during late active labor when the going got rocky. Andy whispered the images of my special place to me. I imagined myself in my special place and that soothed the pain and gave me strength." Here are the steps the mother can follow:

· Get into a comfortable position and relax.
· Breathe deeply and rhythmically, and imagine each breath you take in as bringing health-giving life energy and each breath out as carrying tension away.

· Continue breathing this way for a minute or so and feel yourself entering a more peaceful, relaxed state of mind and body.

· Now imagine that you are in a special place that is peaceful and makes you feel secure and comfortable. It can be any place at all, real or imaginary—a favorite room; a beautiful, natural setting; in a meadow; near a bubbling brook; by the ocean—anywhere you feel completely safe and comfortable.

· Let the details of this special place unfold.

· Take a few minutes to explore this place and enjoy it.

· Acknowledge that this is your own place. No one can enter without your invitation. You can return here at any time and feel peaceful and completely relaxed.

· Take a deep breath and when you are ready, count slowly to five and open your eyes.

Once the mother has created a special place of her liking, she can share the details of this place with you. Then during labor, when she is uncomfortable and less in control than she is now, you can lead her through guided imagery to this special place and help her relax.

The Radiant Breath

The "radiant breath" exercise is very effective when contractions get rough or in the presence of discomfort or tension. In this exercise, guided imagery works hand in hand with rhythmic breathing.

The mother should do this exercise a few times during pregnancy to get the feeling for it, and the childbirth companion can guide her through this during labor. Here are the steps the mother can follow:

- Take a deep breath in and let it out.
- Imagine that with each breath you take in, you are breathing in a soft, golden, radiant light.
- Imagine that you are breathing this light directly into your womb, where it surrounds your baby with health-giving energy.
- As you continue to breathe in this radiant light, imagine that it wells up to fill your entire body, your whole being.
- Let the radiant light expand and grow until it radiates out from you in all directions, surrounding you with a beautiful golden aura or halo.
- If you wish, direct the light to any part of your body that feels tense or uncomfortable.
- Imagine a million fingers of radiant light massaging away the tension or discomfort.
- When you are ready to return to the world of everyday life, take a deep breath, count slowly to five, and open your eyes.

Chapter Four

. . . .

HELPING HER EVERY STEP
OF THE WAY: EARLY LABOR

This chapter covers the basics of helping the laboring woman from the moment labor begins until labor becomes active (when the cervix is dilated to 5 centimeters or more). This chapter and chapter 5 make up the heart of this book. The chapters can be read in advance of labor or you can use them if you are just picking up this book for the first time during labor.

More often than not, labor's onset takes the mother by surprise. Labor may begin 2 or more weeks before or after the expected due date. For this reason, to avoid rushing at the last minute, the childbirth companion should be prepared at least 2 weeks in advance. Preparation before labor will enable you and the mother you are supporting to be more relaxed and ready for labor.

Emily, whose labor began early, remembered: "My labor started with a shout a full 10 days before my due date. I was so relieved that I had prepared for labor and packed my stuff for the hospital in advance. There were no horrid surprises. We had everything ready to go."

WHAT TO DO BEFORE LABOR BEGINS

My wife, Jan, and I thought we were prepared for labor. But we hadn't expected a change of hospital. During labor, we changed physicians because our physician was away for the weekend and we hadn't met his backup provider. By changing to a doctor we knew and admired, we changed hospitals. I was unfamiliar with the route to the hospital and we had one nervous ride getting there, wondering if we would arrive on time. You can easily arrange for the items on the following list before labor begins to make things as smooth as possible:

- Be sure there is plenty of gas in your car.
- Be sure you are acquainted with the route to the hospital or birthing center.
- Install an infant car seat for the ride home if you are planning on giving birth outside the home.
- Make arrangements for someone to care for any siblings.
- Plan for help around the house for the time after the baby is born.
- If planning a hospital or birthing center birth, be sure everything the mother wants with her during labor is packed (see the next section).

- Be available for the mother to reach you at all times via cell phone or pager.

Packing for the Hospital or Childbearing Center

If you are planning an out-of-home birth, be prepared with things to pack at least 2 weeks in advance of the expected date of birth. All of the items on the following list are optional. Be sure the mother has with her the things she will want during labor and for the first hours after the baby is born:

- Watch with a second hand to time contractions
- Cold fruit juices and/or a thermos with hot tea to drink and hard candy to suck on when the mouth gets dry
- Pen and paper to make notes about labor's progresses
- A favorite picture or other object to use as a focal point for concentration
- Favorite washable robe
- Lip balm
- Oil for massage
- Warm socks
- Camera and film
- Food for the childbirth companion
- Swimsuit for the childbirth companion to shower with the mother if giving birth in the hospital
- Phone numbers of people to call when the baby is born

- Cassette player and tapes of relaxing music
- This book

Here are some items to pack for the time after birth:

- Nightgown that opens in front for ease in breast-feeding
- Nursing bras
- Clean underwear
- Shampoo, shower cap, hairbrush, and other related items
- Pocket money for food or anything else you might need
- Clothes to go home in (usually maternity clothes)
- Baby clothes, diapers, and receiving blankets to take the baby home in
- Infant car seat

Preparing for a Home Birth

If you are preparing for a home birth, be sure all of the following items are available at least 2 weeks before the mother's expected due date. Your physician or midwife may give you a list of addition items:

- A waterproof pad or shower curtain to prevent staining the mattress
- Two sets of sheets, one for birth and one for after
- Large disposable pads to place under the mother during labor
- Clean washcloths for compresses

- Clean towels
- Tea and/or plenty of other fluids to drink

WHEN LABOR BEGINS

When labor begins, there is usually plenty of time to get ready. The beginning of labor often comes in the night without warning, though there are usually signs. However, rest assured: there is almost always plenty of time to give labor support and plenty of time to get to the birthplace if the mother is planning an out-of-home birth. Babies are rarely born in cars. When labor first begins, there are a number of things you can do:

- Try to get plenty of rest yourself for your demanding role ahead.
- Call the mother's physician or midwife.
- Arrange for child care if the mother has other children.
- Be sure everything is packed.

HELPING HER THROUGH EARLY LABOR

During early labor, the cervix dilates to 3–5 centimeters. This is the longest phase of labor. Progress is slow, but contractions are usually easily manageable.

Increased vaginal discharge is common. The mucus plug from the cervix may be released if it hasn't been already. Membranes may rupture or leak.

The mother may be excited, talkative, and nervous when labor begins and may want to spend time with you, sitting and talking, watching television, going for a walk, and so on. The mother will probably be able to do light activities.

Your role is not as demanding during early labor as it will be during active labor and transition. But you can share most, if not all, of early labor with the mother. You need not be with her every minute unless you both want to be together during this long phase of labor. If she is like most women, she will not need your help continually.

If labor begins during the daytime, the mother can continue her daily activities. Light activity is a good way to keep the mind off labor. Should labor begin at night, which happens more often than not, the mother can rest. However, she may be far more comfortable keeping busy, taking a shower or bath, or reading than just lying down and waiting for the next contraction. The following sections go over some things you can do during early labor.

Be Prepared to Help 2–3 Weeks before the Due Date

If you don't live with the mother, make arrangements for her to call you as soon as labor has begun. Be sure you have a cell phone close by you at all times.

Shelby, a woman who gave labor support to Diana, said: "Diana did not call me until labor was under way. She just did things around the house until she was unable to continue with daily activity. Then once labor got going, I came to her home and assisted her. I would have been there through early labor but she didn't need my help."

Heidi woke her husband, Jake, at the first sign of labor. "We wanted to share the whole experience," Heidi recalls. "I didn't need Jake's help as much as I did during active labor. But having him with me was great! He timed contractions, made me a chicken salad sandwich, and kept me walking around the house. When labor grew more active, we set off for the hospital. We snuggled in the car all the way to the birthplace. I really needed to lean on him."

Time a Few Contractions

The intensity, frequency, and duration of contractions gives you an idea of how labor is moving along. As mentioned, uterine contractions become stronger and last longer as labor progresses.

To time the length of a contraction, use the second hand of a watch. The mother will tell you when the contraction begins and ends. Or you can feel the uterus tighten by placing your hand gently on the mother's abdomen.

To time the frequency of contractions, measure from the beginning of one contraction to the beginning of the next one, and not, as you might suspect, from the end of one to the beginning of the next. For example, if contractions occur at 7:00, 7:05, 7:10, 7:15, and so on, and each one lasts 60 seconds, then they are 5 minutes apart even though the actual rest period between contractions is only 4 minutes.

It is unnecessary to keep a written record of contractions throughout labor. In fact, doing so distracts you from giving the support the mother needs. However, you may want to keep a record in the beginning of early labor to determine whether the mother is experiencing true or false labor.

Contractions will probably come in a pattern, and a glance at your watch will tell you when the next one is due. Some mothers like to be told when their contractions are beginning, peaking, and tapering off. They might also like to be told when a contraction is almost over. Others find such continual reporting annoying. They cannot work with their body and surrender to labor if they are waiting for the clock to tell them when the next contraction is coming.

"Teddy timed a few contractions just to see where I was at during labor," recalls Leia. "I didn't want him going overboard and keeping a labor record like they advised us to do during childbirth class. In my opinion, that just distracts the mother from labor. Some guys time contractions throughout labor. This is for the birds! The purpose of timing contractions is to get an idea of where you are at during labor. Is it early labor, active labor? How far apart are the contractions? How long do they last? You only need to time a few contractions to answer those questions."

Suggest That She Get Rest

If labor begins at night, the mother may want to try to get some more sleep before contractions make that impossible. She may be too excited to go back to sleep. If she cannot sleep, encourage her to take a warm shower or bath or do energy-conserving activities. She may be far more comfortable keeping busy than just lying down and waiting for the next contraction.

Holly, whose labor began in the middle of the night, said: "I woke up at 2:30 am with contractions. I was so excited I couldn't go back to sleep! I got up and took a long, relaxing bath. Then I went out with my husband, Andy, for a wee-hours-of-the-morning walk. When I returned home, I took a shower even though I was spotlessly clean. I stood under the warm water for what seemed like an hour. Then contractions picked up and Andy supported me through the rest of labor."

Encourage Her to Continue with Daily Activities

If labor begins in the daytime, the mother can continue whatever she normally does until she is sure that she is really in labor. If she is up, be sure she doesn't tire herself out with too much activity.

Kathrina said of her early labor, "When labor started out with mild contractions lasting 20–30 seconds and occurring every 20–30 minutes, I continued cooking. I cooked a full meal before I felt the need to relax. Labor's contractions were coming closer together and lasting longer. I took a walk with

Luke and then showered and got ready for birth. I was so excited I was going to give birth. I was too excited to rest. I did, however, practice relaxation with Luke touching tense areas of my body and telling me to let go of tension to his warm touch. When labor got active, we shifted to the childbearing center where we gave birth to our daughter, Crissy."

"I went shopping during early labor," recalls Tansy, who gave birth to her two children in a hospital. "During my first labor, contractions were too mild to bother with needing to rest. They were occurring every 20 minutes or so and lasting about a half minute. My cervix was 4 centimeters dilated before early labor began, and it was 6 centimeters when contractions started coming every 5 minutes. I bought the full week's supply of food and carried the bags to my car. Suddenly contractions started coming in earnest and labor was getting serious. I rushed home and into my husband Sam's arms. After a few minutes of rest, I put the food away with Sam's help. Then when contractions were occurring every 5 minutes, we left for the hospital. During my second labor, contractions started out at 12–10 minutes apart and lasted about three-quarters of a minute. This was no time for doing the week's shopping! I watched a couple of DVDs before labor got really under way, with contractions every 3–5 minutes and lasting about 60–75 seconds. At that juncture, Jake took me to the hospital. I was 7 centimeters dilated."

Serve Easily Digestible Foods and Liquids

The mother will need nourishment for the demanding work of labor. Good foods and liquids during labor include chicken soup, gelatin desserts, fruit juices, tea with honey, and so on. The mother's own desires should be her guide about how much she should eat and drink.

The custom of withholding all food and liquid from laboring women is peculiar to some American hospitals. It began when women were put to sleep for birth to avoid the possibility of suffocation caused by aspiration of the contents of the stomach. Today, because general anesthesia is avoided in all but the most serious emergencies, the custom of withholding food and drink is falling by the wayside.

Nancy, who labored in a hospital with restrictive policies, explained: "The hospital wouldn't let me eat or drink. All they would give me is ice chips. This is no fare for a laboring woman! She deserves her favorite drink and her favorite foods. My fiancé, Adrian, smuggled in a canteen of cranberry juice. He gave me some to drink when the nurses were out of the room. I highly recommend that you have a canteen of your favorite fruit juice or a thermos with hot tea with you at all times during labor."

Lucy, who labored in a hospital once contractions became active, said: "I spent early labor at home. David prepared me potato soup and oyster crackers with a glass of fruit punch. It was just what I needed to go on my way through early labor.

During active labor, hours later, I wanted to drink fruit juice but I didn't want to eat anything at all."

Remind Her to Urinate at Least Once Every Hour

Reminding the mother to urinate may seem like ridiculous advice. But she may not feel the urge to empty the bladder as labor progresses. A full bladder can impede labor's progress and contribute to unnecessary discomfort. If you wish, note the time that she urinates to let you know when to remind her.

Tessa said, "I didn't sense the need to empty my bladder. There seemed to be no sensation to urinate on account of labor. Slim told me to go the bathroom and urinate at least every hour. Though I didn't sense the need, I produced water. It made me feel more comfortable."

Suggest She Take a Walk

Walking will hasten labor's progress. The effect of gravity will help dilate the cervix and shorten labor. When a contraction occurs, put your arms around the mother and let her lean on you. She should stop walking only if walking is uncomfortable or if birth is imminent.

After 11 hours of irregular contractions, some weak, some strong, Linda went to the hospital to find she was only 4 centimeters dilated and still in early labor. She said: "Kenny and I left the hospital and walked downtown, hoping labor would pick up. When I didn't feel like walking any more, I took a shower and let the warm water spray on my lower back. This was very relaxing and soothing. Afterward, instead of lying in bed and just waiting, we went out and walked around again. The fresh air made me feel good, and walking helped the contractions come faster and stronger."

Debra said, "I really wanted to walk during early labor. My husband, John, and I went for a short hike in the mountains. The country air and the sights and sounds of our walk were exhilarating. We hiked about 3 miles. After the hike, we took a long country drive. All the way I was thinking this hike and drive were preparing me for the big event of birth. I was in early labor about 10 hours before contractions got really intense."

Karen, who labored without medication, said: "My husband, Roger, remained with me throughout early labor. We took walks and watched DVDs. Then when labor become more dominant, he massaged me and talked me through contractions."

Keep Her Upright, If Possible

Sitting, standing, or kneeling encourages shorter, easier labors with more efficient contractions. Help the mother avoid remaining in bed unless it is night and she is sleeping.

Andrea, who labored with on and off contractions for about 24 hours, shared this: "Carol, my labor support person, reminded me to kneel during contractions when I was too tired to walk around. It helped stabilize my contractions during a long labor. When I was too exhausted to kneel I sat in a rocking chair."

Lauren, who stayed at home until labor got active, said: "I was too uncomfortable to go walking around. Paul, my husband and childbirth companion, insisted that I not lie down unless I really felt the need. I stayed upright, alternating sitting in an easy chair and standing. When I was standing up and a contraction came, I threw my arms around Paul's neck and leaned on him for support. I am convinced that the upright position hastened labor's progress."

Suggest That She Take a Shower or Bath

The woman may find taking a shower or bath relaxing. Of course, she should not take a tub bath if membranes have already ruptured.

"I never found a shower more soothing," said Miranda, "or more necessary. I didn't use soap. I just stood under the shower, letting the warm water course over my belly and my back. Ryan showered with me for some of the time, but after a while he got sick of it. I still showered on. It helped me through the last part of early labor and the first part of active labor. I only got out of the shower when Ryan said if I didn't hurry up and go the hospital, I would have an unplanned water birth."

"During early labor, I took a long, warm tub bath," stated Belinda. "It felt good to be in the bath. Tony didn't need to help me yet so I was alone. When labor got active, I took another bath and this time, Tony poured warm water over my abdomen. It was soothing during contractions."

Help Her Relax

Early labor is a good time to practice the autogenic stress release described in chapter 3. Practicing relaxation during the early phase will help the mother relax when labor becomes more active and she is more prone to tensing up.

You can also put your hands on a tense area and tell her to relax to your touch or to let go of tension, feeling it flow away to your hands.

Crystal Lee, who labored in a childbearing center since her contractions began, recalled: "We went to the birth center at the very beginning of labor because it was such a long drive away. I wasn't worried about laboring in a foreign environment because the birth center was so homey and didn't have any restrictive policies; we could do what we wanted. During early labor, we practiced autogenic stress release so I could carry a sense of deep relaxation through the rest of labor. Harris, my husband, spoke the suggestions to me as I followed. 'Your right arm feels warm and heavy,' and so on. We had practiced this form of relaxation during pregnancy, and in labor it was second nature. When labor got active, we no longer had time for these lengthy suggestions. Harris just told me to relax my arms if they were tense, or my legs if I had contracted muscles in my legs and I did what he suggested. Labor was not difficult.

I think that was partly due to the homey environment and mostly due to my relaxation."

Nicole, a new mother who gave birth at home, has this to say: "Shamus and I practiced relaxation during pregnancy so it was easy to relax during early labor. I could sense that being relaxed helped my contractions be less painful and more efficient. Whenever I felt a part of my body like my jaw tense up, Shamus put his fingers on either side and told me to release tension to his touch. That was especially good when I clenched my teeth, which I did often during labor. Shamus was there with me touching my jaw and telling me to relax my mouth. I had heard that a relaxed mouth meant a relaxed birth outlet so I made a special effort to release tension when he told me to."

Call the Mother's Physician or Midwife

You should call the mother's physician or midwife to inform him or her that labor is under way and you are reasonably sure it isn't false labor (see the section on true and false labor in chapter 2).

Martha and James, a couple who spent early labor at home and went to the hospital only when labor became active, said, "We waited until labor was fairly well established before we called Martha's doctor to tell him the good news. Contractions were coming every 15 minutes and lasting 45 seconds. We waited because we didn't want to be stuck in the hospital during early labor. We learned that sometimes in hospitals, the clock is set in motion. That means if we don't labor actively within a certain frame of time—I'm not sure when that is—Martha would have her labor augmented with drugs. We didn't want that. We had learned that an augmented labor is far more painful than a natural labor. The long and the short of it was, we waited until we were sure labor wouldn't stop before calling the physician."

Margaret, who gave birth in a hospital quite a drive from her home, said, "We called our midwife at the first sign of labor. We wanted to be sure she was ready and that we would be getting her and not some backup that we hadn't met. As soon as we were sure it was the real thing with contractions every half hour, we made that dramatic phone call. I'm glad we did because we had a long drive to the hospital and much of labor was spent in the car."

Contact Anyone Who Will Be Attending the Birth

Be sure to give whoever is attending the birth plenty of time to get ready. "I was frustrated during early labor," remarked Cyndi, a third-time mother. "Our two daughters were staying at my mother's house. It was the middle of night when I called my mother. I couldn't convince her that labor was moving along quickly. She wanted to let the children sleep another few hours. I was beside myself with anxiety because I wanted my children to witness the birth. We had prepared them for what to expect during pregnancy and they were eagerly looking forward to being at the birth. My mother was convinced that, since I was in early labor, I would be in labor for several hours more and that there was plenty of time. I told her there wasn't plenty of time and she had to leave now! She still was taking her time leaving the house. Finally, my husband, Francis, called and shouted at her. 'Leave now! Or you will miss the birth!' She still took her time. She arrived with the kids just in time to see Erika born. She missed the end of first-stage labor and arrived during the middle of second stage, which didn't last very long. At least she arrived. I was grateful that the children witnessed the birth of their baby sister."

Amy Lee and Jim, the parents of a new baby boy who was born in a hospital, recalled, "We didn't waste a minute. As soon as we knew that labor was real and not false labor, we phoned our parents and my two sisters. They were planning to attend the labor and birth with us. They rushed over to our home and accompanied us to the hospital. I was overjoyed that I had so many relatives attending my birth I felt really secure and at peace knowing there were familiar faces present."

Make Arrangements If the Mother Has Other Children

If the siblings will be attending the birth, make sure someone is there to care for them so they won't get tired or tire out the mother.

"We planned on having our son and our daughter attend the birth," recalled Mandy about the birth of her third child.

"At the first sign of a contraction, I called Penny, my sister, and asked her to arrive at our house soon. She was the support person for my son and daughter. She prepared to mind them through labor because they are 6 and 7 years old and couldn't stay cooped up with me throughout what might turn out to be a long labor. They required someone to see to their needs, to come and go with them when labor got boring for them, and to show them how they could help me when contractions waxed strong. Harry, my husband, and I, had a wonderful family birth at home with the children and my sister present."

On giving birth to her fourth child, Amelia said, "I expected my labor to go quickly because I had given birth three times before. I called the kids' nanny as soon as I knew I was in labor. She was expecting a midnight call to tell her when to care for the kids. I didn't want to take any chances so I phoned early rather than wait until the last minute. She came by and took care of the kids just as we were heading for the hospital. I labored for only 5 hours and gave birth to Jo-Ellen, my new daughter."

Be Sure Everything Is Packed for the Birthplace

Emily, a first-time mother, planned to give birth in a child-bearing center: "We waited until the very moment I had to go to the birth center to pack our stuff. This was a big mistake. We were rushing around like crazy getting things together. It made me anxious during labor and could have caused my labor to go awry. I strongly urge every expectant parent to pack well in advance of their due date."

Unlike Emily, Miranda packed early and well in advance of labor. "We had fruit juice, a robe for me to wear during labor, a cassette player with tapes of my favorite music, and lots of other stuff packed 3 weeks before my expected date of birth. I felt reassured when we had packed early. I know that a mother can go into labor 2 weeks or more before her due date and didn't want any hassles running around looking for stuff during labor."

Get Rest Yourself

You will need your energy for the big event. Bear in mind that you may be awake all night or for more than a night depending on how long the labor is.

"We took a nap together, Celia and I," recalled Michael, who helped his partner give birth in a local hospital after a long labor at home. "We didn't sleep soundly, but even a fitful sleep filled with dreams is better than no rest at all. We were all rested when early labor grew more intense and it was time to call our midwife. Harder contractions woke her up. She tried not to wake me so I would be rested for my role ahead. But I woke up the second she got out of bed. I was too concerned about helping Celia to get any more sleep."

WHEN TO LEAVE FOR THE BIRTHPLACE

If the mother is planning on a hospital or childbearing-center birth, you are probably wondering about the best time to leave for the birthplace. This depends on the distance you must drive; the recommendations of the physician or midwife; and, above all, the mother's preferences.

As a general rule of thumb, the mother should labor at home for as long as possible. This is particularly true if hospital policies restrict her from doing what she wants, such as walking about and coming and going as she pleases. Dana said of her early labor, "I stayed at home throughout labor's beginning and until I really couldn't control myself anymore. I felt most secure and comfortable and in control at home."

Lennie stayed home throughout most of active labor. "I felt most comfortable at giving birth in the hospital, but I was more at ease laboring at home until the last minute. I felt more secure in my own space." Although one mother may labor better at home, another may let go and labor naturally only when she is in her chosen birthing environment.

If there is a great distance between home and hospital or child-bearing center, the mother may want to leave early. According to Kitty, "We had about an hour's drive to the hospital. So I left for the hospital during early labor. I wanted to be in the hospital where I would be giving birth as soon as possible."

Bear in mind that an unfamiliar environment may slow labor

down. In general, the best time to leave is when contractions last about 1 minute and occur at about 5-minute intervals.

ADMISSION TO THE HOSPITAL

Remain together during hospital admission procedures. Fill out any forms you can in advance of labor so the mother will not have her concentration interrupted when she needs every bit of her strength to get through labor.

Upon admission to the hospital, the mother is escorted to the labor or birthing room. She is often brought to the room where she will be laboring by wheelchair. However, if she prefers to walk, she can decline the wheelchair. The mother may feel that sitting in a wheelchair is reminiscent of being sick—during labor, she is radiantly healthy, not ill.

In the labor room, she will be given a hospital gown to wear. Some mothers prefer their own familiar clothing and will bring a favorite robe. Other mothers prefer to wear the hospital gown rather than getting their own clothing soiled.

A nurse will ask the mother several questions. Among other things, she will ask about the frequency and duration of contractions. You can answer for the mother if she doesn't feel like talking or is having a contraction. This is where timing a few contractions comes in handy.

A vaginal examination is done to assess labor's progress. If the cervix is dilated only 3–4 centimeters and if no further progress is made in an hour or so, the mother may prefer to go home and return to the birthplace when labor becomes more active.

Labor may slow down or stop altogether upon admission to the hospital. This is probably the result of anxiety in the unfamiliar birthing environment. Remember that labor is an emotionally sensitive process and the mother's feelings about her birthing environment will influence contractions. You can alleviate the mother's negative feelings about the birthing environment and help labor progress more smoothly if you do the following:

· Help her relax.
· Try guided imagery, particularly the "special place" exercise (see chapter 3).
· Massage her shoulders or back to release tension and make her feel good.
· Guide her through slow breathing.

Emmy, a new mother of a baby boy, spent most of active labor in a hospital with her husband, Dan. "Dan was familiar with the images of my special place. He told me to relax and imagine that I was lying on that cool carpet of moss, hearing the birdsong, smelling the fragrance of the country air, and listening to a bubbling brook. It was amazing how much that relaxed and put me at ease in the noisy environment of a tertiary care center. I was able to focus on the images of my special place instead of the sights and sounds of the hospital. It felt great."

In some hospitals, a nurse will remain with the mother throughout labor. Some mothers appreciate this. Claudia said: "The nurse was great! She encouraged me and helped my husband, Rich, by putting cold compresses on my forehead while he massaged my back."

Other mothers prefer to be with their childbirth companion alone. If this is the mother's preference, don't hesitate to tell the nurse that the mother would rather be alone. Donna, who labored in a hospital, said: "I wanted to be alone with my husband, Donald. The nurses were probably very helpful, but I didn't want anyone else present during my labor. It was an intimate experience only to be shared by me and Donald."

Whether the mother goes to the hospital during early or active labor is entirely up to her and her health-care provider. If she feels like going to the hospital early to get settled right away or because she lives a long way from the place of birth, be prepared to practice relaxation and guided imagery with her to counter the effects of the environment. If she decides to wait until labor becomes active because she feels more comfortable laboring at home, be sure that she has done whatever admission procedures she can in advance. In either case, with your help, she will be better able to labor in harmony with nature.

Chapter Five

. . . .

HELPING HER EVERY STEP
OF THE WAY: ACTIVE LABOR

This chapter covers helping the mother through labor from the moment that the cervix is 3–5 centimeters dilated to the time the baby is born. Your support is vital as labor progresses. You need not follow every suggestion to give effective labor support. Be flexible. Do whatever most helps the mother. For example, some women like to be touched, caressed, and massaged through labor. Others don't like to be touched and prefer more verbal support. If the mother you are supporting doesn't like to be touched, don't take it personally. This is just the way labor unfolds.

There is no right or wrong way to help a woman through active labor and birth. Every childbirth companion has his or her own style. The most important thing is sharing the mother's experience with her and being a nurturing, caring presence.

You—the childbirth companion—are as fully important as any other member of the health-care team. As discussed earlier, you can help the mother relax, reduce her fear and pain, reduce the length of labor, decrease the likelihood of a Cesarean section or other complications, reduce the chance of complications relating to the newborn, and enhance parent-infant bonding. This is true whether or not you've had previous experience with childbirth.

During active labor, the cervix dilates from 3–5 centimeters to 7–8 centimeters. Contractions last 45–75 seconds and occur at intervals of 5–3 minutes.

The uterus works increasingly hard during this stage. Contractions become more intense. Membranes may rupture and then be followed by a sense of relief. The mother may feel pressure in the hips and legs as the baby descends deeper into the pelvis.

THE MOTHER'S REACTION

As labor progresses and contractions come more frequently and are more intense, the mother will depend on you for almost-continuous support. She usually becomes more serious and more involved with her labor at this stage. She begins to find concentration, attention to her breathing, or guided imagery and labor support more essential. She can continue walking if at all possible. Walking increases the efficiency of contractions. Most women report less pain while upright than while lying down.

Your support becomes more important and your role

becomes more demanding during active labor. You needn't follow every single suggestion in this chapter to give effective labor support. Just be flexible and follow whatever suggestions seem to be most helpful to the mother. For instance, some women like to be touched, caressed, and massaged throughout labor. Others prefer more verbal support. What works for one woman may not work for another.

Martha recalled: "During active labor, I needed Brian by my side, helping me through contractions. He told me when a contraction was beginning, when it was at its height, and when it was dying away. He helped me stay sitting or standing, rather than lying down which helped my labor to move along. When I took a bath, he poured warm water over my uncomfortable belly. When I sat up in a rocking chair, he massaged my shoulders and talked me through contractions. His help was invaluable."

Janice said: "Dan led me through a guided imagery during late labor. I found this very relaxing. It helped me marshal my inner resources and enabled me to cope with labor when the going got rough. We used my special place that I had practiced during pregnancy. Dan reminded me of the scenes in my special place and helped me imagine that I was comfortable, secure, and at peace. I found this much more helpful than controlled breathing, though I tried to keep my breathing slow and regular." The following paragraphs share some ways to help the mother through active labor.

Share her experience. Don't sit passively nearby like a detached observer. Get right on the bed with her if she is laboring on a bed. Walk with her if she is up walking. Be as actively involved as you can while you follow the other suggestions here.

Help her stay relaxed. This is your foremost task. Relaxation is key to a more efficient labor. Relaxation during contractions is essential to avoid unnecessary pain and tension. Encourage her to let her body go limp. Of course, if she becomes tense, just telling her to relax does little good. Helping her relax a specific part of the body is far more effective. Place your hands on a tense area and stroke or massage it, asking her to relieve tension to your touch. For example, should she make a fist and tense the muscles of her arm, stroke her arm with both hands from the shoulders to the fingers. Pay special attention to the face, legs, and arms. Also, if she curls her toes, massage her feet and legs. If she grinds her teeth, touch either side of her jaw and massage lightly with your fingertips. Try to remain calm yourself. The mother will find it difficult to relax if you are tense.

Guide her with regulated breathing patterns if she is using them. Remind her to take a cleansing breath—a deep breath in through the nose and out through the mouth—at the beginning and end of each contraction. This assists some women in relaxing and signals the childbirth companion that a contraction is occurring.

Guide her with her breathing. Make eye contact and remind her of the breathing patterns if she is using them. Laboring women often forget what they have learned in childbirth class and practiced at home. Breathe with her if she finds it helpful. Your partner may feel like using slow, rhythmic breathing to help her through active labor. She may also want to use an external focal point—a picture, a favorite object, your face—to fix her attention during contractions. Some women prefer to focus inward with closed eyes, visualizing the cervix opening or the baby moving downward during contractions. Do not insist that she breathe in a certain way if she does not find it helpful.

Encourage her to relax deeply as she exhales with each cleansing breath. Watch for signs of hyperventilation, such as tingling hands and light-headedness, especially if she is breathing rapidly. If she does hyperventilate, suggest that she breathe more slowly and try to relax. You can advise her to breathe into cupped hands or a paper bag (rebreathing her own exhaled carbon dioxide) for a few breaths. Help her to breathe more slowly and relax during future contractions.

Breathe with her. You can breathe with the mother if she has difficulty managing through a contraction. This is an effective way to help her remain calm and avoid panic. Some couples prefer to breathe together throughout labor, the labor partner tapping the rhythm of the mother's breath on her arm or leg or simply keeping up eye contact during the breathing. Others prefer to breathe together only when necessary. Experiment until you find the style that suits you best.

Guide her with guided imagery. Guide her through one of the guided imagery exercises from this book or whatever other exercise she has planned to use. Use a soft voice, pausing after each step to give her plenty of time to complete the image. Repeat the same guided imagery exercise or vary exercises from contraction to contraction, whichever the mother prefers.

Encourage her to feel free to vocalize as she feels the need. As labor progresses, some but not all mothers may moan, groan, and sigh. This is perfectly normal and indicates that the mother has elicited the laboring mind response (see chapter 3). Deep, low moaning and groaning help dissolve tension and fear and better enable the mother to surrender to labor.

Encourage her to continue walking if at all possible. Walking increases the efficiency of contractions. Walk with her. During a contraction, let her lean on you with your arms around her.

Encourage her to stay in an upright position. Most women report less pain when upright than lying down. Have her sit up in an easy chair or a rocking chair, if one is available, or have her kneel or stand.

Use warm water to help her relax and ease her discomfort. Apply hot compresses to the area of discomfort, abdomen, groin, lower back, and so forth. Thoroughly wet a towel or washcloth with hot water and wring out excess water. Change compresses often to keep them warm. You can also help her take a warm bath. Draw a bath with water as deep as possible if the mother's membranes still haven't ruptured. Bathing soothes labor's discomfort. You can also pour water from a glass or pitcher over her abdomen during contractions.

Help her take a warm shower. Many women find the spray of the shower relaxing. They may want to stand in the shower with water running down their back or abdomen or both. Feel free to take a shower with her. You can support her with your arms around her during contractions.

Make her comfortable. There are many things you can do to make sure the mother is comfortable. Adjust her bed and place pillows wherever she desires. Wipe perspiration from her face and neck. If she wants, place cool, moist washcloths on her forehead. Be sure she has ice chips or hard candy to suck on and cool water, fruit juice, or hot tea always handy. Her mouth may get very dry, especially if she is using rapid mouth breathing.

Establish eye contact during contractions. This lets the mother know you are with her emotionally and helps her feel less alone in her labor.

Maintain physical contact. Touch, caress, or massage her—whatever she prefers. Lock eyes with hers when things get difficult. Tell her you love her. This is reassuring and comforting to many mothers. Others don't like to be touched toward the end of labor. Let the mother's comfort be your guide. Laughter always helps, too. Every labor can benefit from lightening up. Between, not during, contractions, ask her if what you are doing is helpful. Find out what will make her feel best. Don't just assume.

Massage her. You can massage her shoulders, arms, back, and legs. When you massage her legs, try stroking with both hands downward from the groin to the ankles and back again with less pressure going from the ankles to the groin.

Be positive in all conversation. The laboring mother is highly open to suggestion. She is particularly vulnerable to negative feelings and discouraging thoughts. Acknowledging the tough contractions and her good effort to stay with them is most helpful. Remind her that the more intense contractions of active labor are probably accomplishing more.

Encourage her to take one contraction at a time. If she is in pain, when the contraction is over, ask her where it hurt. Some women say, "All over." Ask her to be specific so you can help. For example, if the discomfort is mostly in the back, you can suggest a change of position or try back counterpressure. If in front, you might try effleurage, massaging her feet and legs, and talking her through contractions.

Avoid negative comments about her behavior or her labor's progress. Encourage and praise her repeatedly even if you think you sound like a broken record, such as by saying, "You're doing wonderfully." During labor this is more valuable than sympathy. Don't feel, however, that you must keep up a continuous conversation. Some laboring women prefer silence.

Don't underrate her difficulty. This will only frustrate her. Tell her that you understand what she is experiencing is very hard.

Give your encouragement and understanding and your reassurance that all is well.

Shield her from outside disturbances. You can dim the lights. If people are talking during a contraction, ask them to lower their voices or wait until the contraction is over. Answer questions for her when appropriate. Let her know it is all right to do her own thing.

Help with back labor. You can help the mother change position. Encourage her to assume a position that alleviates the pressure of the baby's head on the spine. Postures that alleviate back labor include the following:

· Resting on hands and knees
· Kneeling with head resting on her arms on your lap or on a chair, bed, and so forth
· Sitting backward on a chair with the head resting on the chair's back
· Lying on her side
· Standing and walking

Apply firm continuous counterpressure to the spine with the heel or your hand during contractions. Adjust the pressure as the mother directs. You can also apply an ice bag or hot water bottle to the area of discomfort.

Let her know that you believe and trust in her strength and power to give birth. A simple reassurance in your confidence in her can help the mother relax into the rhythm or her labor or find the strength to cope with especially intense contractions.

Help her to relax the pelvic floor. Suggest visualizing the birth pathway opening more and more with each contraction. This is precisely what is happening, but it sometimes helps to be reminded of the fact. Perineal massage or holding warm washcloths against the birth outlet often feels good to some women and aids relaxation.

Ask her for feedback about what you are doing. Is it helpful? Would she like to try something else? Tailor your support to her needs.

TRANSITION (LATE-FIRST-STAGE LABOR)

This section covers transition, the final phase of active labor and the bridge between first-stage labor and the second stage, or birth. Transition is usually the most difficult but the shortest phase of labor. If membranes haven't ruptured, they probably will have by the end of transition. Transition is the final phase of active labor. Many women find this to be the most difficult, but shortest, part of labor. Others do not notice a distinct transition phase. The laboring mother will be quite dependent on her birth partner at this time. The birth partner should try not to leave her, even for a short while.

During transition, the cervix dilates from 7–8 centimeters to 10 centimeters. Contractions last from 60–90 seconds and occur at 2–3 minute intervals. They may have two or three peaks and be irregular in strength, frequency, and duration. During transition, the mother may experience any or all of the following:

- Trembling legs
- Hiccuping or long, loud belching
- Nausea and vomiting
- Inability to remain comfortable
- Alternating hot and cold spells
- Irritability
- Restlessness
- Fogginess
- Increased pressure
- An urge to push before being fully dilated
- Not wanting to be touched

Transition is often marked by confusion and a variety of emotions: discouragement, despair, frustration. At times, the mother may lose control, feel overwhelmed, and even cry. She needs your continuous support. Try not to leave her alone even for a short while.

As the cervix dilates the final 2–3 centimeters, the mother may feel as if the tremendous power of labor has taken over her body. She may feel nauseated or vomit. You can do nothing but provide a basin for her to use and be by her side. Her legs may tremble. Inner-thigh massage and heat applied to the groin will help her stop trembling. When the time to give birth draws, you may hear a "catch," a soft grunt in her breathing, or she may begin holding her breath. This indicates she is involuntarily bearing down.

She may feel a premature urge to push. But she should not push until the cervix is fully dilated and the urge to bear down is irresistible. Tell her to breathe through the urge by breathing out through pursed lips as if blowing out a candle. Although her body continues bearing down, by breathing in this way she can keep from bearing down involuntarily.

Toward the end of first-stage labor, she may have a powerful urge to move her bowels. This is caused by rectal pressure from the baby's descent in the pelvis. It is a positive sign. Birth is near.

Occasionally, the rim of the cervix remains undilated, especially if the mother has been lying in the same position for some time. Should this occur, help her remain relaxed and change position. She should avoid pushing unless her healthcare provider suggests otherwise. Sometimes bearing down in an upright an upright or squatting position can push the rim of cervix out of the way.

Her attention also narrows during this stage. She may be introspective and wholly involved with labor.

Four essential things to remember about giving support through transition are the following:

1. *Physical contact.* If it helps, touch her, caress her, smooth her

hair and let her know you are there at her side. Remember that some women don't like to be touched toward the end of labor. Ask her if she finds physical contact helpful or irritating.

2. *Eye contact.* This will keep her focused on the here and now and remind her that you are there to share her experience.

3. *Encouragement and praise.* Emotional support is more important when the contractions get rough than in any other part of labor.

4. *Keeping her comfortable.* Use cool washcloths on her forehead, give her liquids or ice chips, wipe perspiration away, adjust pillows, help her change position, and so forth.

In addition, to help the mother through transition, keep the following in mind.

Be positive. Don't react if she expresses negative feelings or seems demanding or ungrateful for your support. Negative emotion, from irritability to depression, is one of the signs of transition. Transition is the most difficult labor phase but also the shortest. She will soon see the baby. Tell her, "Everything is going as it should. Labor will soon be over." Her health-care provider or a nurse can be most reassuring to her at this time if she is worried that something is wrong. You can also stay positive by continuing to use all the support measures from the preceding section.

Be firm if necessary. The laboring mother experiences an altered state of mind. Her concentration narrows. You may have to establish eye contact and repeat your instructions simply and firmly.

Adapt to a new way of communication if necessary. The mother's way of expressing herself may change toward the end of labor. During early labor, she might enjoy talking. During transition, she may prefer grunting or nodding to words.

Encourage her to express herself freely and make whatever sounds she wishes. She may feel like moaning, sighing, and groaning. This will help her relax and cooperate with labor. Such sounds do not necessarily indicate pain but are often the laboring woman's natural form of expression. Screaming, however, probably indicates panic and possibly pain.

Help deal with panic. If the mother becomes panic stricken and overwhelmed with fear or begins to scream, sob uncontrollably or thrash about, you can establish eye contact and be gentle but firm. For example, if she is screaming, suggest that she lower the pitch of her voice and moan or groan (a lower-pitched sound often dissolves the panic). Groan with her if that's what she needs. You can also have her breathe with you. Say, "Breathe like this," and then demonstrate. If you or the mother are worried at any time during labor that something may be wrong, or you just want to be reassured that labor is going well, ask a nurse or the health-care provider.

HAVING CONTROL DURING LABOR

In preparing for birth together, your goals are to enable your partner to flow smoothly through labor, to manage the stressful parts, and to participate fully in the birth. But don't expect your partner to maintain perfect control. This is both unrealistic and unnatural.

Control in labor is relative because labor is overwhelming physically and emotionally. Some parts are enjoyable and some parts difficult and stormy. If the mother stays attuned to what is happening rather than fighting the awesome power, she will avoid much discomfort and delay.

Several natural childbirth films give inappropriate pictures of birth, with rigid and precise technique and undaunted self-control. For most women, it is better to respond to contractions by going with the flow rather than going through labor with a grin-and-bear-it attitude.

Reinforce your partner's confidence in her ability to birth naturally and work with her contractions, but don't make it seem as if she is performing an athletic feat. She is not running a race but participating in the miracle of creation. A woman should be free to express herself the way she feels best about letting her emotions go: moaning, sighing, groaning, laughing, or crying. Encourage her to let go and flow with the power that will birth her baby. Allowing yourself to express your own feelings will show her it is all right for her to do the same.

Chapter Six

HELPING HER EVERY STEP
OF THE WAY: BIRTH
(SECOND-STAGE LABOR)

This chapter covers giving support and participating during birth (second-stage labor). During the second stage of labor, the cervix is fully dilated (10 centimeters). Contractions last about 60 seconds and occur at varying intervals of 5 to 2 minutes. The baby descends through the birth canal and is born.

Second-stage labor is entirely different from first-stage labor. Contractions are usually not as uncomfortable. They demand that the mother bear down actively. The mother usually feels the urge to push several times during each contraction. She pushes with the urge, which usually intensifies as the baby moves down the birth canal.

Typically, the mother experiences renewed energy and excitement and may feel afraid when the head is crowning. Most women find the birth process the most enjoyable part of labor. Others find the second stage difficult and uncomfortable. In any case, your support is still important during this exciting stage of labor.

It may take some time, perhaps even an hour, before a laboring mother gets used to the feeling of pushing and lets herself be swept up in the urge to bear down. Sit near your partner as she bears down. For many women, the urge to bear down is irresistible. For others, the urge is not as pronounced, particularly if they have used medication.

Enjoy the birth process as you help your partner. This is the most exciting and dramatic part of labor. Everyone gets involved. But don't forget to help her during all the excitement. The following sections suggest some ways for you to help.

Help her change position. You can help her change position if she wishes or if she needs to do so to enhance progress. Your partner can bear down in whatever position she feels most comfortable and can change position as often as she likes. You can also help by reminding her to keep her shoulders rounded while bearing down and not to throw back her head or arch her back, which can be uncomfortable and waste energy. You might help her squat, kneel, or sit up for a few contractions.

Some health-care providers are skilled at delivering babies only when the mother is in a reclining or semi-reclining position, If this is the case with her health-care provider, the mother can adopt whatever position she wants during most of second stage and then switch to the position that the health-care provider prefers when birth is imminent. Here are some common positions for second-stage labor:

- Semi-reclining with the head and shoulders well supported. This is comfortable for most mothers. However, if the baby is in a posterior position, resting on her back may be uncomfortable.
- Lying on her side. This is a good position if she is tired or has had epidural anesthesia and has little control of her legs. You can hold the mother's top leg up during pushing.
- Resting on hands and knees or kneeling on pillows with her head on your lap.
- Squatting on the bed or the floor. In this position, the birth outlet is slightly shortened, the pelvic outlet expanded, and gravity is working for the mother. Squatting can often shorten an overlong second-stage labor. Try this position if the baby does not seem to be making any progress. You can hold the mother's hands and support her as she bears down. She can sit up or go forward on her hands and knees between contractions.
- Standing or semi-squatting with knees slightly bent. You can support her with your hands under arms as she bears down.
- Sitting on a toilet. Unappealing as this may sound, it gives the mother a physical advantage and is particularly helpful for a long second-stage labor. She moves elsewhere once the baby makes progress down the birth outlet.

Help her relax between contractions. She may fall into a dreamy half-sleeping, half-waking state of mind. Second-stage labor is hard work. Wipe perspiration from her brow and place cool washcloths on her forehead. Keep her environment as serene as possible. Instructions from the health-care provider and nurses may be necessary. However, if your partner does not want enthusiastic coaching throughout second-stage labor, let her wishes be known. Tell the staff that you would both prefer to give birth in quiet. Dim the lights. Ask people to be quiet if their talking disturbs the mother.

Help her to relax her pelvic floor. Many mothers resist the sensation of birth by tightening the buttocks or drawing up the pelvic floor muscles, which will prolong second-stage labor and contribute to the possibility of tearing. Merely telling a mother to relax her pelvic floor is not always effective. Help her relax her mouth instead. A loose mouth usually reflects a loose bottom. She may find warm compresses or a washcloth to the perineum soothing. You can also try perineal massage with oil. During contractions, you can remind her to push in the direction of the warmth.

Interface with the obstetrical staff. Convey the health-care provider's instructions to the mother and the mother's questions or concerns to the staff. In some hospitals, nurses give enthusiastic coaching throughout second-stage labor (such as "Push, push, push!" "That's it!" "Keep it coming!"). Some mothers like this type of coaching. Others find it a nuisance. If your partner does not like this, tell the obstetrical staff that she prefers to bear down in silence and to push with the natural urges of her own body.

Encourage her to imagine herself opening for the baby. Try a guided imagery exercise. Encourage your partner to welcome the unfamiliar sensations of birth and to let go. This may be difficult at times. Be patient. The mother may feel tremendous pressure during this part of the birth process. She may find the sensations of second-stage labor alarming. Reassure her that all is going well, that what she is feeling is normal, that her body was designed to stretch around the baby, and that these sensations will soon pass.

Let her know when you first glimpse the baby's head in the birth outlet. This is an exciting milestone of second-stage labor. You will probably see her enthusiasm double when you make this announcement, especially if it is a long second-stage labor.

Remind her to reach down and touch the baby's head. The mother can reach down and touch the baby's head when it appears large enough for her to do this. This is another exciting milestone of second-stage labor.

Hold a mirror so she can watch the birth. But don't insist she watch if she doesn't want to. Some laboring women find observing an aid to enjoying the miracle of birth, but others find it irrelevant or even frightening.

When the head crowns, assist her to breathe the baby out. Forceful pushing at this time may result in tearing. The health-care provider will give instructions. Repeat these to your partner. If your partner gives birth in a bed in a birthing room or at home, you may be able to catch the baby or assist the midwife or physician in doing so.

Try to minimize the last-minute commotion. When the birth becomes imminent, if your partner is in a hospital with a labor or delivery room arrangement, she will be wheeled to the delivery room when the head begins to show, usually about as large a fifty-cent piece for first births and about the size of a dime for subsequent births. The move from one room to another during the second stage is unnecessary and can be traumatic. It should be avoided whenever possible.

Ask if your partner can give birth in the labor room. Some, if not most, hospitals allow this. If she must give birth in the delivery room, ask if she can remain in her bed for birth rather than being moved to the delivery table, which is both unnecessary and traumatic. Otherwise, in the delivery room, the mother is moved from her bed to a delivery table. Her feet may be placed in stirrups, which is also unnecessary and should be avoided if at all possible; the perineal area is washed with an antiseptic solution; and her legs are draped, leaving only the birth outlet exposed.

In the delivery room, you will probably have to wear sterile hospital clothing and maybe a mask, more unnecessary customs that are fortunately falling by the wayside. Try to change into your sterile clothing as early as possible to avoid last-minute rushing about. Avoid touching the sterile instruments, which will be arranged on a table within easy access of the physician or midwife.

When the baby's head crowns (when the largest diameter of the head passes through the birth outlet), your partner may momentarily panic and feel as if she is burning or tearing. Assist her in breathing the baby out. Suggest that she breathe through pursed lips to avoid bearing down.

Help her avoid tearing. Her body was meant to stretch around the baby and give birth with little or no tearing. To help her, you can do the following:

· Hold hot compresses to the perineum (area between the vagina and the anus) between contractions.
· Do perineal massage during contractions until the baby's head shows. It is not necessary to wear gloves for this, but make sure your hands are clean.
· Help your partner assume a comfortable birthing position.
· Help her avoid bearing down actively as the baby's head is being born.
· You can suggest that she try guided imagery exercises.

Help her avoid an episiotomy. An episiotomy (a surgical incision to enlarge the birth outlet) is warranted only if there is a problem with the baby and birth must take place quickly or if a large maternal tear seems inevitable without the incision. This incision makes postpartum recovery far more uncomfortable and should certainly be avoided. To help your partner avoid an episiotomy, follow the preceding suggestions for avoiding tearing. Unfortunately, some health-care providers routinely perform episiotomies, especially for first-time mothers. The mother who wants to avoid an episiotomy must take on the responsibility of choosing a health-care provider who will do one only when warranted.

If you plan to catch the baby, be sure to let the health-care provider know in advance. Catching the baby as he emerges slippery and wet from the mother's body can be a beautiful and unforgettable experience. My wife, Jan, and I did this when our boys were born.

The health-care provider usually guides the birth of the head (which most requires expert supervision); then the birth partner can put out his or her hands to catch the baby. The mother can also reach down and take her child with her hands, one under each of the baby's arms, and lift the child to her breast. Make sure your hands are thoroughly washed. It is not necessary to wear gloves, though most birth attendants do. The health-care provider will probably stand by to assist or instruct you and to make sure there are no complications. After birth, place the newborn on your partner's abdomen. This way she can take the baby to her breast whenever she wants.

THIRD-STAGE LABOR

Third-stage labor, or the delivery of the placenta, usually lasts only a few minutes. Contractions occur at regular intervals, but the mother may not even notice them in the excitement of getting to know her child. The placenta usually separates after the third of fourth contraction. Breast-feeding helps the process.

The mother will be asked to bear down with or one or more contractions to birth the placenta. The umbilical cord is usually cut before the placenta is delivered. The mother can get up any time after birth as long as she takes it slowly. She should first sit up, then rise gently. Support her so she doesn't fall. When she first gets up, some blood may escape after having accumulated in the vagina.

Your partner may have mild to laborlike contractions for a while after birth. These pains are more pronounced if medication has been given to contract the uterus after subsequent births and during nursing. The contractions are beneficial in that they help prevent postpartum bleeding. You can help her relieve the discomfort by reminding her to empty her bladder. A full bladder makes it difficult for the uterus to remain contracted, so it may keep contracting and relaxing, causing discomfort. You can also suggest that she lie face down with a pillow under her lower belly. The pressure will keep the uterus contracted. Pains may get worse for a few moments before being relieved. She can also massage her uterus, just as the nurse or midwife will do whenever he or she finds the uterus relaxed.

You can cut the umbilical cord yourself. Many fathers cut the umbilical cord. Like the exchange of wedding rings or other tokens, cutting the umbilical cord can be a beautiful symbolic gesture of love and welcome. If you do want to cut the cord, let the health-care provider know in advance. A family member or friend may also want to cut the cord.

The beautiful, bluish white cord is curly, like the receiver wire of a telephone. One end is attached to the baby and the other to the placenta inside the mother. Of course, cutting the cord does not hurt either the mother or the baby. The cord will continue pulsating for a while after birth as blood passes from the placenta to the baby. Clamping and cutting should be delayed until the pulsing ceases, unless there is a medical reason for doing otherwise. The health-care provider will first prepare the cord by clamping it on either side of the place where it is to be cut. The cord is then cut with a pair of scissors. The cord cutting signifies the end of pregnancy and the welcoming of the baby to your family. During the cord cutting, you and the mother may want to say a prayer of welcome or some other words that you feel are appropriate.

TAKING PHOTOGRAPHS

Some parents want photographs taken during labor, birth, and/or the period shortly afterward for a wonderful addition to the family album. If the mother wants more than a few photos, it is best for a friend or relative, not the father, to take them. Being behind a camera can distance the father from giving his full attention to his partner during labor and from participating in and fully enjoying the birth.

The room should not be brightly lit during labor or, if so, only for short periods. Use high-speed film. Or if you use a direct flash, do so sparingly because this may annoy the laboring mother and hurt the newborn's sensitive eyes.

Chapter Seven

HOW TO HELP HER IN THE FACE OF MEDICAL INTERVENTION

This chapter explains how the father or other birth partner can interact with the mother if she has pain relief medication, anesthesia, intravenous feeding, or electronic fetal monitoring. The birth partner's actions may be limited if the mother has these medical interventions. However, the birth partner's support-giving role should not be minimized.

All forms of medical intervention, such as intravenous feeding and electronic fetal monitoring, and even the clinical setting itself can impair labor's progress and lessen the mother's confidence, which, in turn, can negatively influence her labor. If medical intervention becomes necessary, the mother will especially need effective labor support. The birth partner can help by blanketing the mother with his or her nurturing presence and following the guidelines in this chapter.

Appropriate medical intervention in labor occurs when a medical complication justifies the intervention—and interventions have saved the lives of many mothers and babies. Routine intervention, however, is unjustified and apt to create rather than prevent problems. According to Dr. G. J. Kloosterman, a professor of obstetrics at the University of Amsterdam, "Childbirth in itself is a natural phenomenon and in the large majority of cases needs no interference whatsoever only close observation, moral support, and protection against human meddling."

Any interference with the natural labor process increases the possibility of complications. If the mother wishes to avoid unnecessary intervention, one of your tasks as her birth partner is to help her do so by interfacing with the obstetrical staff and communicating her preferences to them.

INTRAVENOUS FEEDING

Intravenous feeding (IV) unfortunately is routine in some hospitals, though this practice is falling by the wayside. In the presence of medical complications, the IV has an important place. It can supply fluid, nourishment, medication, and blood replacement if the mother is in danger of hemorrhaging. During normal labor, however, the IV should be avoided. It impairs the mother's mobility and is no substitute for taking food and liquids by mouth.

If the mother does not have a medical complication and does not wish to use an IV, explain her position to the obstetrical staff as tactfully as possible. If the mother must have an

IV, request that it be on a mobile stand. Don't be inhibited about touching or interacting with her simply because the IV is in place.

ELECTRONIC FETAL MONITORING

The electronic fetal monitor (EFM) is a machine that records both fetal heart rate and the intensity of uterine contractions on a continuous sheet of graph paper. There are two basic types of monitor: internal and external. With an external monitor, two straps attached to a nearby machine are placed on the mother's abdomen. On one, an ultrasound device picks up the fetal heart rate. On the other, a pressure-sensitive device detects the intensity of contractions. With an internal monitor, a wire is passed through the vagina and cervix and attached to the baby's scalp to pick up the fetal heart rate. A fluid-filled, pressure-sensitive catheter is inserted into the uterus to determine the intensity of contractions.

In some hospitals, EFM is used only for a short while or intermittently. If all appears normal, the monitor is removed. In other hospitals, EFM is used throughout labor. If there are complications, then EFM is useful. However, according to the National Institutes of Health, "Present evidence does not show benefit of electronic fetal monitoring to low-risk patients. EFM impairs the mother's mobility and is associated with increased incidence of unnecessary Cesarean section."

The EFM shows when a contraction begins, peaks, and

tapers off. Some mothers and birth partners find this information useful in coping with contractions. If EFM is in use, do not get caught up with the machine. Many birth partners and health professionals tend to ignore the mother and pay attention to the machine. Sit with your back to the monitor, if necessary. Also, adapt your support to the mother's less mobile position. Don't be inhibited about touching her simply because a machine is in use. Work around the monitor straps.

USE OF PITOCIN

Pitocin, a synthetic form of the hormone oxytocin, which regulates uterine contractions, is sometimes given to the mother intravenously to induce or augment (speed up) labor. Pitocin-induced or augmented contractions are usually more tumultuous and more painful than normal labor contractions. They seem to rise to a peak sharply rather than building up gradually.

Pitocin is one of the most abused of all obstetrical medications, in that it is frequently prescribed before other less intrusive means of inducing or augmenting labor are tried first. A typical scene frequently accompanies the injudicious use of Pitocin. The mother's contractions are slow to dilate the cervix. Pitocin is administered via IV. The contractions become more painful and difficult to manage. The mothers request pain relief medication. The medication slows her contractions further. More Pitocin is administered. Finally, fetal distress is recorded and the mother is wheeled to the operating room for a Cesarean section.

To avoid this scenario, first try all other methods to induce or augment labor besides Pitocin. (See "Inducing an Overdue Labor" and "If Labor Stops or Slows Down.") If, however, the use of Pitocin is necessary to help labor progress, your support will be especially important to your partner. Use all the methods in chapter 5 to reduce discomfort and to help your partner relax, and don't leave her even for a short while if she seems to be having a difficult time.

PAIN-RELIEF MEDICATION

A wide variety of medication is available for use during labor, from tranquilizers taken orally to pain medication such as Demerol administered by injection and epidural anesthesia, which numbs the body from the waist down.

The decision to use pain medication during labor should always be the mother's. Only she knows what she is feeling or whether she needs pain relief. Do not insist that your partner go without medication or that she use medication if she doesn't want to. No mother should be made to feel guilty for taking medication to ease her discomfort. Nor should you feel that you have failed to give good support if your partner should opt for medication.

However, you should be aware that all forms of pain medication impair labor's progress and can prevent the mother from fully participating and enjoying the birth and the wonderful mother-infant bonding immediately afterward.

If a nurse or the health-care provider suggests medication and your partner is committed to going without it, explain her preference and tell the nurse or health-care provider that you will let him or her know if the mother changes her mind.

Before resorting to medication, try everything else you can to relieve her discomfort: guided imagery, slow and deep breathing, a change of scene, a change of position, a soothing shower or bath, back rubs, hot packs on the groin and abdomen, verbal encouragement, and so forth.

Also, before resorting medication, find out how dilated the mother is. If she in transition, birth will occur soon and there won't be much time for the medication to take effect. See her through those final contractions.

Sometimes when a laboring woman asks for pain medication, she is really looking for reassurance. Remind her that she has been handling her contractions well and can continue to do so. If in doubt, ask a nurse or the health-care provider for reassurance that everything is going normally.

If you have tried all of the foregoing and the mother still wants pain medication, then it may be time to consider it. The use of medication during labor is a subject of controversy. Most proponents of natural childbirth point out that no medication has been proven entirely safe for the baby. Medication, many midwives and childbirth educators believe, should only be used as a last resort if a laboring mother needs it. Most people agree that the final choice about medication is the mother's. Only she knows what she is experiencing, and a laboring woman should not feel guilty for taking medication to ease her discomfort if she feels it is necessary.

Chapter Eight

. . . .

SPECIAL SITUATIONS

It was a little past 3 a.m. when we left our home for the birth of our first child. Jan's contractions were coming with crippling intensity every other minute. Walking down the stairs was difficult. We stopped three times when the force of her contractions immobilized her. Once on the front porch, there was only a short distance to the car. Nothing further could interrupt us—so we thought.

We were stepping off the last step when Jan gripped my arm. "Wait—I can't go on," she said. Another contraction. Her uterus went hard as marble.

I embraced her as a cool night breeze swept over my face. Then my eyes widened in horror and my muscles froze. We were prepared for labor but never expected a complication like this! It would have unnerved even the most seasoned physician.

A skunk stood no more than five feet from us. I met the skunk's eyes in the black night. The skunk turned slowly and deliberately before lifting its tail toward our faces.

Jan saw it, too, but she appeared not to notice. She was too involved in her labor to care. When I nudged her to turn back, she whispered, "I can't move."

In the split second between furious heartbeats, I drew her into my arms and carried her up the stairs and away from the skunk. We stood safe behind the plate-glass door of our porch and watched while it slowly walked away. Then we continued our night journey.

Fortunately, encountering a skunk during active labor is rare. A couple need not prepare for the adventure. But every couple should know that labor does not always proceed smoothly. Unforeseen problems may arise. Yet in most circumstances, the birth will still be a joyful, shared event.

Labor does not always progress smoothly. Complications in labor occasionally arise. Your presence and help can make it easier for the mother to cope and sometimes even alleviate or correct the problem.

Amy and David's second child was 3 weeks overdue. During second-stage labor, the baby's heart rate dropped below the normal limit for an unspecified reason. Their physician was concerned the baby was in distress. "Take a couple of deep breaths for the baby," he told the mother.

"I was so involved in my labor," Amy recalls, "that I didn't realize anything was wrong until I saw tears rolling down David's cheeks. At first I thought he was crying because he thought I was in pain. Then I realized he was afraid. The baby wasn't getting enough oxygen. A nurse asked me to roll on my left side (to relieve uterine pressure on the major vessels). I was lying on my side moaning when an oxygen tent was brought up to the bed. This apparently helped. The heartbeat picked up. Then everything happened very fast. David held up my right leg as I pushed. When the head was out, I rolled over onto my back. As soon as the baby was partially born, the midwife turned him and told me to look. The baby was looking straight at me with his eyes wide open. David put one hand on the baby's back and I placed my hands on his head and we completed the delivery ourselves. Our son Graham was born healthy a second later. I was so relieved, smiling, crying."

WHAT TO DO IF LABOR SLOWS DOWN OR STOPS

On occasion, a labor that has been progressing smoothly slackens. Contractions wane in intensity or even cease altogether. The cervix stops dilating. There are numerous causes for this, such as improper use of pain medication, cervical tightness, the mother's age, and emotional factors. If the baby's head is too large for the mother's pelvis, labor may fail to progress and there may be a need for a Cesarean section. Sometimes the cause is unknown. Contractions that dwindle away are sometimes merely evidence of false labor. If this is the case, the cervix will not have dilated (see chapter 2).

In hospitals the most common means of augmenting a flagging labor is either by artificially rupturing the membranes or by giving an intravenous hormonal solution of Pitocin, which regulates uterine contractions. Pitocin is a synthetic form of oxytocin, the hormone the body makes during labor. This procedure can create a more painful and less manageable labor for the mother. Fortunately, there are several ways to accelerate a slackened labor before resorting to the use of intravenous hormones.

For example, if the mother is still in early labor it is not necessary to do anything. There is no hurry. Wait until contractions pick up again. If she is in active labor (more than 4 centimeters dilated) and contractions stop, she can either rest and wait to see what happens or you can try the following.

Encourage your partner to walk around. Walking will help dilate the cervix by way of gravity and may be just what she needs to get her labor going.

Suggest a hot shower. Showering will get your partner into a standing position, increasing pressure on the undilated cervix, and will take her mind off labor, which may help if emotional factors are the cause of the failure to progress.

Help her to relax and get comfortable. Sometimes labor stops because the mother is too tense.

Try love making and/or nipple stimulation. This will help the mother to release her own store of oxytocin, the labor-regulating hormone. Intercourse is contraindicated if the membranes have ruptured (because of the possibility of infection). But kissing, hugging, and fondling the breasts are effective ways of making her feel sexual.

Should the use of Pitocin be necessary, your support is especially important. Contractions may be much more difficult. Use every means of helping your partner relax. You can ask her health-care provider if Pitocin can be started at a slow rate and remain as slow as possible. A fast drip rate may cause contractions that are overwhelming and inappropriate for the particular phase of labor.

If contractions are strong and not dilating the cervix, tension may be the problem. Try everything you can to help her relax: turning off the lights, a warm bath, giving her a back rub, and so forth.

PREMATURE LABOR

Premature labor occurs when labor begins before 37 weeks of gestation (full-term labor is 40 weeks), or 3 or more weeks before the expected due date. Though premature birth is uncommon, it may occur. Be available for the mother to reach you at all times. If you leave your home for an extended period, be sure the mother has a telephone number to reach you or is able to contact someone who can reach you within a short while.

The mother's health-care provider should always be informed immediately if labor begins more than 3 weeks early. The mother's health-care provider may attempt to stop premature labor with bed rest and, if necessary, drugs. If bed rest is prescribed, the birth partner can keep the mother company as time allows and meet her needs at home.

If premature labor seems inevitable, take the following steps:

· Call the mother's health-care provider.
· Drive the mother to the hospital.
· Follow the suggestions in chapters 4 and 5 for helping her through labor.
· Using guided imagery, deep rhythmic breathing, relaxation, and other comfort measures in this book are preferable to pain-relief medication, which can depress the premature baby's heart rate and respiration

AFTER THE BIRTH

Because the baby may need immediate pediatric attention, the parent-infant bonding process may be interrupted or delayed. The postpartum adjustment period can be much more diffi-cult after premature birth because plans have been radically changed—particularly if the birth takes place much earlier than expected. Mother and infant are often separated. The parents may go home while the infant may have to remain in the hospital until his or her condition stabilizes. Your practical help and emotional support can make the rough transition to parenthood much less rocky.

To help in the process, encourage your partner to spend as much time as possible in the intensive care unit with the infant as soon after the birth as possible. This will enhance parent-infant bonding.

You can also give extra time and attention to your partner after the baby is born. Encourage the mother to breast-feed as well. To nurse successfully, the mother must have the encouragement of her partner and/or birth partner. Premature babies especially need their mother's milk. If the baby is too premature to breast-feed, the mother can use a pump and then bottle-feed. Most hospitals provide a breast pump and sterile containers.

If the mother has difficulty coping or wants additional information, contact a support group such as Parents of Prematures.

INDUCING AN OVERDUE LABOR

Labor begins on the due date only 5 percent of the time. Normal labor may begin 2 or more weeks before or after the baby's due date. If labor is a little late getting started, there is usually no cause for concern. However, if labor is long overdue or if there are other medical complications such as maternal diabetes, inducing labor may be warranted. Occasionally, labor does not seem to want to get started at all. If the baby is at term (ready to be born), the health-care provider may want to induce labor.

The two most common medical methods of inducing labor are artificial rupture of the membranes (bag of waters), sometimes referred to as amniotomy, and the intravenous administration of Pitocin. The former method consists of inserting a plastic hook or instrument through the vagina and cervix and breaking the membranes. This is quite painless and sometimes works especially if the cervix is ripe (or effaced and somewhat dilated), and if the baby is low in the pelvis. But this does not guarantee that labor will begin. In addition, the procedure carries the disadvantage of setting the clock in motion, so to speak, because most hospitals insist that birth take place within 24 hours after membranes have ruptured. Induction by means of Pitocin is similar to augmentation and may result in more tumultuous and less manageable contractions.

Both of these methods carry risks. Artificial rupture of the membranes, though painless to the mother, removes the amniotic fluid that has cushioned the baby's head. The increased pressure on the baby's head and umbilical cord may cause fetal distress, which may result in the need for a Cesarean section. In addition, in many hospitals, the mother is expected to give birth within 24 hours once the membranes have ruptured to avoid increased risk of infection. The use of Pitocin usually causes more painful and more tumultuous contractions and it too is associated with a greater risk of fetal distress and Cesarean section.

Before her first child was born, Nancy's bag of waters broke but labor didn't begin. More than 24 hours had passed when her physician decided to use Pitocin to induce labor. Of her induced contractions, she remembered them as "incredibly strong. They seemed to start at the peak. The labor was very difficult. I couldn't have managed without Kenny, my husband.

I had been up all night and I slept between contractions. Kenny sat on my bed and kept his hand on my belly. As soon as he felt a contraction begin, he woke me to tell me to take a cleansing breath. Without his help, I would have lost control."

The following less intrusive, natural, and far more pleasant means of inducing labor should be tried before resorting to medical induction. Check with the mother's health-care provider to be sure there are no medical reasons to avoid any of the following methods:

· Take the mother for a long walk, preferably uphill and downhill. Walking is an effective way to speed up a flagging labor and may initiate contractions by putting pressure on the cervix.

· Serve spicy, gas-producing foods (such as chili, pizza, and carbonated beverages). The intestinal activity may trigger contractions, but no one know precisely why.

· Try love making and/or manual or oral nipple stimulation and if possible bring her to orgasm. Nipple stimulation causes the hormone oxytocin to be released. Orgasm sometimes initiates contractions when the cervix is ripe and the woman is ready to go into labor. Semen contains a substance called prostaglandin that, when it comes into contact with the cervix, stimulates the uterus to begin contracting. Orgasm also may initiate contractions). Do not have intercourse if the bag of waters has already ruptured. Do not stimulate the nipples for more than a few minutes, as prolonged nipple stimulation has been associated with fetal distress.

· Have her take a long shower or take a shower with her.

· Discuss with the mother her concerns about giving birth or becoming a parent. Sometimes a woman can unconsciously hold back her labor if she has strong negative emotions or fears.

Staff persons at Gifford Memorial Hospital in Randolph, Vermont, often recommend a natural form of induction affectionately known as beer, pizza, and orgasm. One mother recalls trying this method: "Our physician suggested we take a long walk together, have pizza and beer, and go home and make vigorous love, 'Bring her to orgasm,' he told my husband. It was hilarious trying to find a position to be vigorous in while nine months pregnant. I thought I would go into labor from laughing so hard." If you decide to try this method, you can substitute a nonalcoholic carbonated beverage for the beer.

IF LABOR STOPS OR SLOWS DOWN

If labor stops or slows down, there is usually no cause for concern. As already mentioned, there are a wide variety of variations in the course of normal labor. Labor may stop for a while along the way, like a hiker pausing to rest midway up a mountain trail. This is perfectly normal.

However, numerous physical and psychological factors can cause a flagging labor, including injudicious use of pain-relief medication, possible disproportion between fetal size and maternal pelvis, maternal tension that may inhibit cervical dilation, and various other emotional factors. It is well known that labor often stops or slows down shortly after the mother is admitted to the hospital. This is presumably the result of anxiety in the unfamiliar environment. Tension between the mother and her partner—or anxiety about giving birth or motherhood—may also cause labor to slow down or even stop altogether.

Sometimes a person in the environment makes the mother uncomfortable and interferes with labor's progress, especially someone who is impatient for labor to move along (like some nurses and health-care providers). The mother may feel she is under pressure to perform, which inhibits her from letting go and laboring normally.

Occasionally, the birth partner inhibits the labor process, particularly if he or she is excessively tense. If this is the case, the birth partner may need to leave the mother alone for a while to give labor a chance to pick up.

The usual medical method of speeding up a flagging labor is the earlier mentioned use of Pitocin to regulate uterine contractions. However, Pitocin usually creates contractions that are more painful and more difficult for the mother to manage. Its use also carries an increased risk of complications, including Cesarean surgery. For these reasons, provided the baby is healthy and there are no other complications, Pitocin should be a last resort to be considered only after other measures have been tried. There are several other measures to try, depending on what phase of labor the mother is in—these are discussed in the following sections.

Early Labor

If early labor contractions have stopped, it is not usually necessary to do anything. The mother may spontaneously resume labor a few hours or days later. However, if contractions are persistent and not dilating the cervix, and the mother has difficulty sleeping, you can try the following:

· Help her relax.
· Suggest that she take a bath or shower.
· Suggest a change of environment or activity (if she in the hospital, consider going home or outside for a while).

Active Labor

If labor slows down during the active phase, try the following:

· Suggest that the mother rest.
· Suggest a change of position.
· Suggest that she maintain an upright position. For most women, labor is more efficient if the mother is sitting, standing, or walking around.

- Suggest a hot shower. This assists relaxation and keeps the mother in an upright position. It may also take her mind off labor for a while, which helps if emotional factors are the cause of slow progress.
- Turn down the lights.
- Try nipple stimulation for a few minutes to release the hormone oxytocin. Do not continue nipple stimulation for longer than a few minutes unless the baby is monitored to rule out the possibility of fetal distress.
- Try love making (do not have intercourse after the bag of waters has broken). Lovemaking also releases oxytocin and is sometimes a good way to get labor going if the mother is comfortable trying it.
- Be sure the mother has adequate nourishment. Encourage her to eat and drink to restore her energy and body fluids.
- If someone in the room makes the mother uncomfortable, ask the person to leave for a while.
- Use guided imagery.
- Talk with her about concerns she may have about birth or becoming a mother. (Sometimes fears about birth or emotional resistance to becoming a parent can cause her to hold her labor back unconsciously).

Prolonged Labor

The length of labor varies widely from a few hours or less to several days with contractions occurring in an on-an-off pattern. Various factors influence labor's length, including the size of the baby, the size and shape of the maternal pelvis, other physical factors, the birthing environment, the mother's feelings about birth, and the presence of a birth partner.

Unfortunately, in some hospitals, mothers are expected to labor and give birth within a certain average time. If they don't, health workers administer Pitocin to speed things up. This is one reason parents should choose a health-care provider and birthplace with staff who accept wide variations in normal labor. Provided the baby is healthy and the mother is not too tired, the best thing to do is forget the clock and let labor unfold naturally. However, if first stage labor seems unduly long and the other is exhausted, try the suggestions listed earlier in this chapter, in the section "If Labor Stops or Slows Down."

For second-stage labor, suggest that the mother change positions. Standing, squatting, or sitting on the toilet all enlist the aid of gravity and sometimes speed up a long second stage. Support the mother if she is pushing in a standing position. If she is sitting on the toilet, have her move somewhere else once the baby begins descending. Try guided imagery exercises as well.

PROLAPSED UMBILICAL CORD

Prolapsed umbilical cord is an extremely rare complication and a grave obstetrical emergency requiring immediate attention to save the life of the baby. The cord prolapses and precedes the baby in the birth outlet; it can sometimes be seen at the vaginal opening. Prolapse of the cord is most common when the baby is in a breech position or when the head is not engaged. It usually occurs at the time of rupture of the membranes or shortly afterward.

Although prolapse is painless to the mother, the baby's oxygen and blood circulation are cut off, resulting in suffocation. The treatment is an emergency Cesarean birth. If you suspect a prolapsed cord, tell the mother to get down on her knees in a knee-chest position with her head and shoulders resting on her arms and her hips higher than her knees. While she remains in this position, call an ambulance and her healthcare provider immediately.

If the cord protrudes from the vagina, gently place a warm wet cloth around it, but only if you can do so without disturbing the cord or the mother's position. Cover her with a blanket to keep her warm, and do not attempt to place the cord back in the vagina or apply pressure to the cord.

LABORING IN A HIGHLY TECHNICAL SETTING

A mother is apt to labor more efficiently if she is in a peaceful birthing environment where she feels safe and comfortable. Laboring in impersonal surroundings can make her tense and impair labor's progress. Interruptions, noise, and the presence of unwanted strangers can inhibit contractions or render them less effective.

Animals instinctively seek out a peaceful environment conducive to labor. Experiments with mice have shown that environmental disturbances can cause labor complications and affect the health of the offspring. Humans, with a more highly developed nervous system, are more susceptible to the influence of their environment than other animals are.

However, for mothers with medical complications, it may be advisable to labor in a highly technical setting. To a degree, the birth partner can reduce the negative effects of a less-than-optimal environment. As birth partner, you can try the following:

· Stay by her side continuously.
· Interface with the obstetrical staff. If the mother is in active labor, answer questions for her.
· Pay special attention to helping her relax.
· Use guided imagery to help her focus on labor.

IF THE BABY DIES

Not every baby is born healthy. Not all babies survive. Not every birth is joyful. Sometimes the baby does not survive. The death of a baby usually can be neither predicted nor avoided.

The death of a baby before or during birth is rare, but it is a reality that does occur. In fact, death is almost invariably the result of causes outside the mother's control, possible exceptions being drug abuse and poor maternal nutrition. It may occur for reasons that the mother can neither control nor predict. Whatever the cause, sadness suddenly replaces joy.

If the baby does not survive, the parents may react in a variety of ways. They usually first feel dazed and numbed by the shock, perhaps unable to believe it. Intense sadness and grieving then takes over. Anger may come and the parents may seek a reason for the death. The parents may go home thinking and dreaming of their child. Everything is a reminder of the baby they anticipated—baby clothes, diapers, cradles, mobiles, toys, and so on. Seeing new parents with their infants, pregnant women, commercials on television, ads in magazines—anything that touches on the reality of parenthood—seems to open the terrible wound still further. The flood of tears seems endless.

Grief is a painful, but essential part, of resolving loss. It is necessary to grieve to go on living an emotionally healthy life. It takes time to grieve the loss of a baby. Only time will reduce the pain of loss. Then it is helpful to plan for the future. Another child cannot replace the child who has been lost. But making future plans gives hope.

Under medically normal circumstances, a couple can try to conceive another child shortly after the postpartum recovery. If there are medical problems, they should consult a physician for advice.

Support from friends and relatives, and especially from people who have suffered a similar loss, can be most helpful. Talking about the baby and how it hurts to have lost the baby is therapeutic, even essential, to both partners through the grieving process.

If you find yourself in such a situation, reach out to each other and to those who love you and care about you. Ask them to help you through this difficult time. Support from the childbirth companion can also be helpful.

If the father is the birth partner, he, too, will be affected by the tragedy. If another person is the birth partner, talk to the mother about the loss: allow her to talk her feelings through. Talking about the baby and how it hurts is therapeutic.

EMERGENCY BIRTH

Babies are rarely born in cars or anywhere other than the planned birthplace. However, on rare occasions, labor may progress extremely quickly or the mother may not recognize the final moments of labor. Emergency childbirth then becomes necessary. The following sections walk you step by step through an emergency birth.

Signs That Birth Is Imminent

- The mother feels as though she must move her bowels (often caused by the baby's descent in the birth canal).
- She says the baby is coming. If she says this, take her seriously.
- The head is visible at the vaginal opening during contractions. To see if the head is visible, gently explain to the

mother that you must check on the baby's progress. Tell her to remove her clothing from the waist down. Help her get into a semi-reclining position with back and shoulders supported by cushions or pillows and legs apart. She should not be flat on her back, as this position will diminish the baby's blood and oxygen supply. Look at the vaginal opening during a contraction. Tell the mother to let you know when she is having a contraction. If this is her first baby and you cannot see the head in the vaginal opening during a contraction, you probably have time to get her to the birthplace or to wait for the health provider to arrive in the case of a home birth. If the head is visible or if the mother insists that birth is imminent, begin preparing for birth as quickly as possible.

Preparing for the Birth

· Remain as calm and as reassuring as possible.
· Get medical help immediately. Call the mother's health-care provider or an ambulance.
· Help her get into the semi-reclining position described in the previous section. This position may slow down the delivery a little and will give the baby a safe place to land.
· Place clean towels or linens under her buttocks. You can put a shower curtain or plastic sheet under her to prevent staining.

· If you are in a car and she feels that birth is imminent, pull over to the side of the road. Put emergency flashers on. Keep the heat running if it is cold outside. Help her get comfortable in the backseat in the semi-reclining position described in the previous section.

The Birth

· Tell the mother to pant through an open mouth during contractions to avoid actively pushing. Let the uterus do the work. This is especially important once you can see the head in the birth outlet and while the head is being born.
· As the head is born, support the head under the vagina with your hand and a clean washcloth.
· If the amniotic sac (the bag of waters, which looks like cellophane) surrounds the baby's face, pull the membrane away from the mouth and nose to allow the baby to breathe.
· Gently wipe any mucus and fluid away from the baby's mouth and nose with a cloth.
· Check to see if the cord is around the neck. If it is, gently lift it over the head before the rest of the body is born.
· When the baby's head rotates to one side, indicating that the shoulders are ready to be born, support the head with your hands. *Do not* pull on the head. When the mother has the next contraction, encourage her to push. Once the shoulders are born, the rest of the body will follow quickly.

The baby will be wet and slippery. Take caution to avoiding dropping him or her.

· Dry the baby and place him or her on the mother's abdomen, face down so the nose and mouth can drain if necessary. Be sure the baby's head is turned so he or she can breathe freely.

If the Baby Does Not Breathe Right Away

· The baby will almost always begin breathing on his or her own. A few babies, however, have difficulty.
· Don't panic. As long as the placenta is still attached, the baby is receiving oxygen from the mother.
· Check the mouth and nose for mucus.
· Vigorously rub the baby's back and/or soles of the feet. If in a minute or two the baby is still not breathing, give infant resuscitation. Cover the baby's mouth and nose with your mouth, placing your fingers on the chest. Gently puff only the air in your mouth into the baby. You will feel the chest rise slightly. *Do not blow hard.* This can cause the baby's sensitive lungs to rupture. Continue puffing at the rate of once every 5 seconds until the baby begins breathing.

Delivery of the Placenta

The placenta usually delivers within a few minutes of the birth of the baby, but first there will be a lull in contractions. At this time, observe the baby to be sure he or she is breathing without difficulty and get the baby to begin nursing.

Be alert for signs the placenta will deliver:

· The uterus contracts (the mother's abdomen hardens).
· A trickle or sudden spurt of blood escapes from the vagina.
· The umbilical cord protrudes three or more inches farther out of the vagina.

Place a container under the birth outlet to catch the placenta as it emerges. *Do not* pull on the cord to delivery the placenta. This can cause hemorrhage. When the placenta is expelled, wrap it in a cloth and place it near the baby. Wait for medical help to arrive if at home. Continue to the birthplace if in a car.

Excessive Bleeding in the Mother

There will be some blood loss after the placenta is delivered. However, if bleeding is excessive (more than two cups) do the following:

· Massage the mother's abdomen 2–3 inches below the navel with a deep circular motion to help the uterus contract and stop the blood flow.

· Put the mother's nipple in the baby's mouth and try to get the baby to nurse.
· If the baby is not nursing, tell the mother to massage her nipples to stimulate the flow of the hormone oxytocin, which helps to contract the uterus.
· Get medical attention for the mother as soon as possible.

Chapter Nine

GIVING SUPPORT THROUGH CESAREAN BIRTH

The Cesarean rate in the United States is one of the highest in the world—more than 27 percent. This unbelievably high rate is a sad reflection on the extent to which a technical approach to birth has replaced a trust in the natural processes of childbearing. The process of birth almost always works best without interference. Cesarean birth is sometimes necessary to guarantee the health of the mother and to save the life of the unborn. But the overwhelming majority of Cesarean surgeries are avoidable. Under normal circumstances, a woman is able to birth a healthy child without major surgery.

Expectant parents can greatly reduce the chance of a Cesarean by laboring in a comfortable environment and choosing a health-care provider who supports normal and natural childbirth and has a low Cesarean rate. According to many concerned health professionals, inappropriate medical intervention increases the possibility of complications leading to Cesarean delivery. For example, the use of electronic fetal monitoring restricts a mother's movements, which, in turn, can affect her labor. Similarly, hormonal induction or augmentation of labor can increase the chance of fetal distress. Avoiding a Cesarean begins with becoming well informed and planning for birth carefully.

Because the Cesarean rate is so high, every childbirth companion should know what to expect during and after Cesarean surgery and how best to support the mother. Whenever possible, it is preferable to take steps to prevent a Cesarean section rather than to cope with the experience afterward. Your help during and after Cesarean birth can:

· Lessen the mother's anxiety
· Help her focus on the birth rather than the operation
· Reduce her discomfort after birth
· Reduce postpartum blues
· Enhance parent-infant attachment

Many birth partners feel uncomfortable, if not downright terrified, at the thought of attending a Cesarean section. You do not have to witness the surgery. During surgery, the birth partner sits at the mother's head, and a screen is placed between her head and abdomen, which blocks your view as well as the mother's.

Because the majority of Cesareans are unplanned, all mothers and couples are urged to choose a hospital that welcomes the birth partner's participation throughout Cesarean surgery and recovery. Every couple should be prepared for the possibility of a Cesarean birth.

REASONS FOR CESAREAN SURGERY

Most Cesarean sections in this country are unnecessary and therefore preventable. Many physicians perform Cesareans whenever there is the slightest question about the baby's well-being or when they feel that labor is not progressing normally. Oftentimes, it becomes clear after the surgery that there was no problem whatsoever.

Cesarean prevention is something for which the parents must take primary responsibility by maintaining a healthy pregnancy and choosing a health-care provider and birthplace with a low Cesarean rate. Such health-care providers are more cautious about performing major surgery. They are willing to take the time to perform additional tests, try other measures, and wait for nature to take its course, relying on surgery only as a last resort. The birth partner, too, can facilitate the smooth progression of a Cesarean by helping the mother relax during labor and by following the suggestions in this book.

Despite the best preparation, a Cesarean birth is sometimes necessary to preserve the health of mother and baby. Legitimate circumstances that sometimes make a Cesarean preferable to normal birth include the following:

- Obstetrical complications such as *placenta previa* (the placenta lies over the cervical opening) or *abruptio placentae* (the placenta detaches prematurely from the uterine wall).
- Maternal illness such as preeclampsia (a disease of pregnancy characterized by high blood pressure, swelling, and protein in the urine), diabetes, or other diseases.
- Fetal distress (a reduced fetal oxygen supply, recognized by certain changes in the fetal heart tones).
- Dysfunctional labor, such as lack of cervical dilatation after all measures have been tried, or cephalo-pelvic disproportion (CPD), meaning that the baby's head is too large for the maternal pelvis, though true CPD is rare because the fetal head bones mold and the bony pelvis is able to stretch somewhat as a result of softening of the ligaments. The most common reason given for Cesarean surgery is CPD.
- Breech baby—most physicians today prefer to deliver all breech babies by Cesarean section, though this is open to controversy.
- Repeat Cesarean, which accounts for nearly one-third of the total Cesarean rate in the United States. Yet several health professionals have proved that many (if not most) repeat Cesareans are unnecessary. Most women who have had a Cesarean can have a vaginal birth in the future if they are willing to look hard enough to find a practitioner who believes in and supports vaginal birth after Cesarean.

Whatever the reason, should your partner have a Cesarean, you can do much to help her. Though a major surgery, a Cesarean delivery is still a birth. And Cesarean birth can be a positive, joyful event.

Every father has a right (a basic human right, not a legal right) to share birth with his partner and support her whether the baby is born vaginally or by Cesarean. Yet many hospitals throughout the country will not allow fathers to be in the room during obstetrical surgery. For this reason, it is strongly recommended that all couples ascertain hospital policy in this regard before choosing where their baby will be born.

THE CESAREAN DECISION

The decision to perform a Cesarean may be made during either pregnancy or labor and for many different reasons. How you and the mother react and how you will be able to help her depend on her particular situation.

Planned Cesarean Birth

Occasionally, a mother knows in advance that she will have a Cesarean section. In this case, there are no surprises. You can plan her birth with her. The mother will have time to think about the type of anesthesia she wants and how she wants you to help her during surgery and immediately afterward. You and she can also plan how you can assist her during the days after the baby is born.

Unplanned Cesareans

Most Cesarean sections are unplanned. The decision to perform surgery is made at the last minute during labor. Usually, however, you and the mother will have some time to talk together. The mother will no doubt feel confused, disoriented, and in need of emotional support. You, too, may be disappointed and shocked.

"My Cesarean was unexpected," recalled Tammi, a new mother. "My partner never left my side. He held my hand and reassured me. Just being with me, he reminded me that my Cesarean was a birth, not just an operation."

Oftentimes, the Cesarean decision is an option. For instance, labor may be too long, the mother exhausted, or the cervix just does not seem to dilate. If there is no sign of fetal distress, the mother may have a choice to continue with labor as it is or opt for a Cesarean. If the Cesarean decision is optional, the mother should be sure to have tried all other means of getting labor going before resorting to major abdominal surgery (see "If Labor Stops or Slows Down" in chapter 8).

If the Cesarean decision seems inevitable, take the following steps:

- Remain with the mother as a nurturing supportive presence.
- Help her to think clearly about her possible options—choice of anesthesia, your presence in the operating room, and so forth.

- Let her express her feelings, her frustration, or her relief at the decision to perform surgery.
- Let her know that, whatever she decides, you are there to help her.

Emergency Cesarean Birth

In the event of a true medical emergency, you will have little time to discuss the mother's options or feelings. You both will probably have done all you can to cope with the moment. Do whatever the medical staff asks you to do, and give whatever emotional support you can to the mother.

ANESTHESIA FOR CESAREAN SURGERY

Two basic types of anesthesia are used for Cesarean surgery: general and regional. General anesthesia renders the mother unconscious. Many hospitals do not permit the presence of a birth partner when general anesthesia is used, though this should always be the parents' choice and policies are becoming more flexible at some institutions. If you do attend when the mother has had general anesthesia, you can witness the birth and share the experience with her later.

Regional anesthesia numbs the mother's abdominal region while she remains awake. Though the mother may feel pressure, tugging, and pulling during surgery, she should feel no pain. If there is pain, she should tell the physician so that the anesthetic can be adjusted. Regional anesthesia may be either spinal or epidural. Both are administered by means of a needle inserted in the back, In the epidural, a thin hollow tube is left in the back for the duration of surgery so that more anesthetic can be injected as needed. Both spinal and epidural anesthesia numb the body from waist to toes and render the area temporarily immobile.

Other forms of anesthesia for Cesarean surgery include local anesthesia, during which just the area of surgery is anesthetized, and acupuncture, an ancient Chinese method involving the relatively painless insertion of needles. However, both these forms of anesthesia are quite rare in this country.

PREOPERATIVE PROCEDURES

Ideally, you should remain with the mother throughout preoperative preparations. This is an anxious time and your presence will make her less nervous. Unfortunately, however, the birth partner is usually asked to remain in a waiting room for about half an hour while the mother is prepared and surgery ready to begin. If this is the case, ask her physician for special permission to remain with her. If you cannot remain, ask to be called as soon as possible.

The following procedures take place—usually in the labor room, sometimes in the operating room—shortly before surgery. First the mother is prepared for the operation. The mother's abdomen is shaved, an IV is started, and a catheter is inserted to remove fluid from the bladder. An antacid is sometimes given to neutralize stomach acids. In many hospitals, mothers are routinely given a sedative. The advantage is a calmer frame of mind during surgery; the disadvantage is grogginess during and after birth for both mother and baby. Whether the mother takes a sedative should be her choice. Discuss her feelings with her. Consider using relaxation and other labor-coping methods instead of a sedative.

Once in the operating room (usually the delivery room), the mother's arms are usually strapped to two boards extending out to each side to prevent her from inadvertently touching the sterile area. The leads to a cardiac monitor are placed on her chest to give continuous feedback about her heartbeat, and a blood pressure cuff is attached to her arm.

Before surgery begins, a screen is placed between the mother's head and abdomen, blocking her view of the surgery. An anesthesiologist administers the anesthetic that numbs the mother from the waist down, and surgery begins. The father may be permitted to remain in the operating room while his partner is being prepared for surgery or he may be asked to wait until preparations are complete. In either case, before surgery begins, he will be requested to sit on a stool at the mother's head behind the screen.

During surgery, your partner will not feel any pain, though she may be aware of pulling sensations especially as the baby is delivered. The birth partner's (especially the father's) presence at this time will no doubt make her feel more secure and as though she is participating in a birth rather than being operated on.

When the baby is born, the pediatrician (who probably will be present) conducts a brief exam, and if the baby is healthy, you will probably be able to hold the infant close to your partner's face so she can enjoy eye-to-eye contact. Should the infant be distressed, he or she will be taken immediately to an intensive care unit. You can follow the baby to the nursery. This way you will be able to provide your partner with an account of the baby's first minutes or hours that she will have missed. Your partner will visit when she is ready to make the trip. Under normal circumstances, you may wish to ask that the weighing and measuring be done in your and your partner's presence.

The mother may be able to nurse in the recovery area. But if she is feeling too weak or tired, nursing may have to be delayed. In any case, you should be with her, helping her to put the pieces together, discussing the baby, and sharing the aftermath of this major life event.

A Cesarean delivery is both major surgery and birth. Understandably, the new mother will be doubly exhausted. She will have more discomfort and a longer recovery period than a woman who has birthed naturally. The new father's help during the hospital postpartum stay and around the house afterward is especially important.

Though the end result of a Cesarean delivery is the birth of her anticipated child, a couple planning a natural birth will most likely meet a Cesarean delivery with severe disappointment. This is especially true if the mother and her partner have never considered the possibility of a Cesarean. Frustration, anger, and grief are normal reactions. The mother may feel she has failed even though the event of a Cesarean is outside her immediate control. Questions may nag her about what she should have done to prevent it. The new mother may also feel cheated, especially if she feels the operation was unnecessary. Facing and talking over disappointments together will help the couple and facilitate the growth of the new family.

WHAT TO DO DURING THE OPERATION

Cesarean surgery takes approximately 1 hour from start to finish, including the stitching after the baby is born. The baby will probably be born during the first 15 minutes. The remaining time is spent stitching the incision. In the meantime, the most important thing for you to do during surgery is to be with the mother—perhaps holding her hand if it is free and sharing the tense moments before her child is born. As already stated, you will be seated behind a screen and unable to view the actual surgery. If you want to view the birth, simply stand up.

One father of triplets born by Cesarean section recalled, "I witnessed the entire thing! It was fantastic!" However, most people prefer not to observe the surgery. As one father put it, "I didn't want to see my wife operated on. But I knew I had to be right there with her to greet our child as he was born."

The matchless emotion that so often crowns birth can be as pronounced for Cesarean parents as for those who birth vaginally. Joy and awe may flood the mother when she first greets her child. One mother recalls, "Seeing our child born was a moment of unparalleled joy." However, the Cesarean mother obviously does not have the same freedom to interact spontaneously with her child as does the mother who gives birth vaginally. You can help her greet her child by doing the following:

· Ask to hold the baby as soon as she has been briefly examined, unless complications require immediate medical attention.

· Hold the baby close to the mother so she can caress the infant with her hands (if they are free) and with her face, kiss her child, smell the fresh odor of the newborn, and enjoy eye contact.

· To maximize eye contact between mother and newborn, cup your hands above the baby's eyes. This may encourage the baby to open her eyes. Otherwise, he or she will keep them shut under the bright lights of the operating room.

· If the baby is taken to an intensive care nursery right way, either accompany the newborn or remain with the mother until surgery is complete (whichever you and the mother prefer). Afterward, the mother can request to be taken to the nursery to spend time with her child.

IN THE RECOVERY ROOM

Shortly after surgery, the mother is taken to a recovery room to remain for 2–3 hours until the anesthetic wears off and her condition stabilizes. Remain with the mother. You can give emotional support and help her spend valuable time with the baby. (Unfortunately, the mother and birth partner are separated in some hospitals when the mother goes to the recovery area, particularly if she is in an area with other postoperative patients. This is yet another restrictive hospital policy that should be rescinded.)

If the mother has had general anesthesia, she may feel groggy for a while, and it may be some time before she wants to see and hold her child. If the mother has had regional anesthesia, her legs may tingle for a while as it wears off. A nurse will probably ask her to wiggle her toes, move her feet, and bend her knees. She may have discomfort ranging from mild to severe at the incision site. Pain medication will help. After a spinal, she may have to remain flat on her back for 8–12 hours to prevent post-spinal headache.

Whatever anesthetic is used, a nurse will check temperature, pulse, blood pressure, respiration, vaginal discharge, and the incision site. She will also periodically check the uterus with a hand on the abdomen to make sure it remains contracted (to prevent hemorrhage at the placental site). Pitocin will probably be added to the mother's IV to stimulate uterine contractions.

The mother will probably be given a bed bath and provided with a toothbrush and mouthwash to freshen up.

PARENT-INFANT ATTACHMENT

In the case of surgical birth, the parent-infant relationship receives a traumatic shock. If parents and baby have been separated, they should be reunited as soon as possible. Provided the baby is healthy, you can help the new mother get to know and bond with her child in the recovery room. Hold the infant for the mother if she is too tired to hold the baby herself.

Mother's reactions during immediate post-Cesarean recovery differ widely. The new mother may be so excited that sleep is the farthest thing from her mind. Christine said of the first hours after surgery, "I talked constantly to my husband and when he went out of the room for a few moments to announce the news to the grandparents, I kept up a steady stream of conversation with the nurses."

Or she may feel drowsy. "All I wanted to do was sleep," another mother recalled, "even though I knew it would be a drag for my husband to sit around and watch me snore."

Cynthia, another post-Cesarean mother, fell into a deep sleep shortly after being taken to the recovery room. "I woke to find the baby nursing at my breast, my husband standing nearby supporting her." If the mother does plan to breast-feed, she should begin as soon as possible.

IN THE POSTPARTUM ROOM

The average hospital stay after Cesarean birth is 3–7 days. During this time, the mother may "room in," or stay with the baby in the same room from delivery to discharge, or the baby may remain in a nursery most of the time and be with the mother during feedings or at other times as the mother desires.

Rooming-in is the best arrangement for the new Cesarean mother because it facilitates breast-feeding, assists in the mother-infant relationship, and helps reduce postpartum blues. Rooming-in needn't be an all-or-nothing affair. If need be, a nurse can take the baby to a nursery to allow the mother to rest now and then. Whatever arrangements the mother opts for, she will need your help. The following paragraphs go over ways to help.

Take on the greater share of baby care (especially important for the father). The mother can and should give care to her child, as this will help her make a smooth transition to new motherhood under the trying circumstances of Cesarean recovery. However, you can help by changing, dressing, bathing, and holding the newborn near the mother.

Help her assume a comfortable nursing position. If she is breast-feeding, there are two comfortable positions. Lying on her side with the baby cradled in the mother's arms facing her and pillows supporting the mother's back, belly, and perhaps upper legs. When the mother has finished nursing from one breast, take the baby and help her roll over so she can nurse from the other. The other is sitting up with knees bent to lessen strain on the abdomen and with a pillow over the stitches. If breast-feeding has been postponed as a result of general anesthesia or the baby's need for immediate medical care, give the mother extra support and encouragement.

Make her comfortable. Adjust pillows and raise or lower the bed as the mother desires.

Remind her to shift her position in the bed often. This is important until she is up and walking about. This enhances blood circulation; promotes healing; and decreases the likelihood of gas pains, a common discomfort of Cesarean mothers.

Encourage her to do abdominal tightening regularly—that is drawing in the abdomen tightly while breathing slowly and evenly. This simple exercise strengthens the abdominal muscles and helps prevent gas pains.

Help her get out of bed and walk around. This is possible within the first 24 hours after birth unless her physician says otherwise. This minimizes the chance of developing blood clots and promotes healing. A nurse will assist the mother her first time out of bed. Afterward, be there for her to lean on you when she walks.

Remind her to stand straight and tall. Though uncomfortable at first, this promotes healing. Cesarean mothers frequently adopt a stooped over posture to protect the incision. But there is no need to worry—the stitches will not pull apart.

HOMECOMING

Whether the mother is discharged from the hospital within 3 days or remains longer before going home, she will need the help of her partner and/or a friend or relative for the first week or so.

The father should take a least a week's paternity leave to be with his partner both in the hospital and later at home. Financial concerns loom large after the baby is born—especially after a Cesarean section, and the father will probably not be paid for the time he takes. However, at this time, his family's emotional needs should take priority. No work is more important than helping your partner.

If the birth partner is a relative or friend, that person should plan to stay with the mother as much as possible and help her out for the first week or so. Enlist other relatives or friends. The post-Cesarean mother has many physical and emotional needs and should not be left to cope on her own. (For specific information about how to help the new mother, see chapter 11, "After the Baby Is Born.")

MEETING SPECIAL NEEDS OF THE CESAREAN MOTHER

The Cesarean mother must recover from both giving birth and having major abdominal surgery. Her sense of dependence and vulnerability is magnified and prolonged when she must adopt a care taking role herself.

A Cesarean section is invariably followed by some degree of *surgical birth trauma*, which is my term for the constellation of physical and emotional problems than can affect the entire family. For example, the physical problems of the Cesarean section include greater discomfort and a longer recovery period than those of the mother who birthed vaginally, increased risk of infection, and other postpartum complications.

Mother-infant separation and its consequences include increased chance of maternal depression, emotional trauma for both mother and baby, and more difficult breast-feeding. The emotional consequences of Cesarean birth may include frustration, disappointment, and grief, which may affect both parents. The unique physical problems of the Cesarean-born baby often lead to a greater need for medical care.

A wide range of normal feelings may follow surgical birth. A few mothers are not particularly concerned with how the baby is born and don't seem upset about having had a Cesarean. But the majority express negative feelings—sometimes profound negative emotions. For those who had hoped, planned, and prepared for a natural birth, a Cesarean section can be emotionally devastating. As June, a psychiatrist, said about her surgical delivery, "I found it difficult to accept the reality of a Cesarean after all those months of preparation for a natural birth. It was an incredible disappointment, a change in everything we had planned."

Many new Cesarean mothers are upset for weeks, months,

and even longer after the birth. Some feel inadequate and wonder whether there is something wrong with their bodies. Many new fathers also feel depressed after a Cesarean. Some blame themselves for having failed their partner, for not giving what they feel was adequate support.

The post-Cesarean period is time to confront these feelings—and to heal. You can encourage the new mother to discuss her feelings about the birth. Let the tears come if necessary. Time, understanding, and support will eventually heal the wounds.

Don't let others minimize the new mother's difficulty—and don't minimize it yourself. Absurd as it may seem, relatives and friends often make thoughtless comments such as, "You did it the easy way," when in fact the Cesarean mother has it harder all around. If relatives or friends suggest that major abdominal surgery is somehow easier than vaginal birth, inform them of the facts.

If the negative feelings are overwhelming or do not abate with time, consult a support organization such as C/SEC. Sometimes it helps to remind the mother that, though a great gulf separates vaginal birth from Cesarean birth, there is also a world of difference between a Cesarean section and any other operation: a child is born.

. . . .

Chapter Ten

GIVING SUPPORT WITH FAMILY AND FRIENDS AT BIRTH

Some couples want their birth to be a private event that only the two of them and their health-care provider share. Others enjoy having several relatives and friends present. They think of birth as a celebration of new life to be shared with those they love. Both experiences can be equally wonderful.

Births shared with family and friends are becoming more common. The presence of relatives and friends can make a laboring mother feel secure. She experiences her emotional highs and lows with familiar faces. For some women, the encouraging voices or simply the presence of trusted friends has a calming effect.

In most out-of-hospital birthing centers, there are no restrictions about inviting guests to a birth. But hospitals vary in their policies as to who may attend. Unfortunately, some permit only one person to remain with the woman during labor, either the mother's partner or a significant other (a friend, relative, or professional labor support person). Other hospitals allow the woman to have one guest or an additional support person along with her partner. And a few have no restrictions about the number of guests with whom the mother may share her birth. But there are still many areas where home is the only place a person can give birth with whomever she pleases present. Find out what your options are if you plan to have family and/or friends present at your baby's birth.

HINTS FOR THE RELATIVE OR FRIEND INVITED TO A BIRTH

Everyone present at a birth is usually drawn into the dramatic event and can find a useful role, even if only speaking a few encouraging words. If you are not actively involved helping or giving physical support, you will probably find yourself participating emotionally. If you are attending the birth of a relative or during which the father will be present, read the section "For the Relative or Friend Who Plans to Give Primary Labor Support" later in this chapter. Although you are not the primary support, much of the same information will be applicable.

Henci Goer, a childbirth educator in San Jose, California, spends a good portion of her class time giving hints about sharing birth with others. She stresses that everyone, even small children, can perform a task during the emotionally and physically intimate experience of labor.

There are many ways to help. If the couple wishes, someone might take photographs when the father of the child has more to occupy his hands and mind than picture taking. You can also offer secondary labor support. You can lend a hand by helping the mother walk; giving her a back massage while the father maintains eye contact and/or talks her through contractions; or replenishing cool washcloths for her forehead, wiping perspiration away, and so forth. You can also relieve the labor partner now and then so he can eat. But don't interfere with the primary partner's support when he is present. The mother can only follow one person's instructions at a time.

At a hospital birth, you can be a patient advocate, helping the couple achieve their goals and avoiding unnecessary medical interventions if this is their desire. But be sure you know what the couple's goals are in advance. You needn't feel shy about speaking to hospital staff and asking for things the parents need—pillows, cool drinks, ice chips, additional washcloths. The staff is there to serve the parents and see that their birth is safe and comfortable. Don't carry on idle conversation in the labor (birthing) room, however. This may annoy and distract the mother.

Practical ways to help at a home birth are looking after siblings; preparing a light meal or beverage for the mother and her partner; changing bedsheets; and cleaning house, doing laundry, and cooking after the baby is born.

Don't feel bad if you cannot find an active role. Bear in mind that a couple may want you to observe and be a guest during this intimate event. Trust your intuition. Many couples will want time now and then to communicate privately. Enter and leave the labor room as it feels comfortable for you and the parents.

A shared birth can be a wonderful family celebration that uplifts all present. Your presence at the birth can both enrich a couple's experience and leave you with a lasting memory.

One couple I know chose to give birth to their child at home. They felt most secure and comfortable there. And it was the only place where they could invite guests to share their birth. The event was like an old-fashioned family celebration. During early labor, Claire sat with her husband, Brandon, on the living room sofa. Her two little girls, aged three and five, played on the floor in front of an oak bookcase. Her mother and sister, a couple who lived nearby, and two midwives who had come to assist were looking at pictures of the little girls and Claire's last birth as they were passed around. One couldn't tell the expectant mother was in labor. She looked so calm and relaxed. Every once in a while, she stopped to take a deep breath. Other than that, her breathing didn't seem to change.

When the contractions grew stronger in the active phase of labor, she took a warm bath. This soothed and relaxed her. Afterward, she and her husband sat on the back porch to enjoy the warm summer evening while the two girls swung on a wooden swing suspended by ropes from a huge pine tree in the yard. The others remained indoors. There was an air of expectancy, as if Thanksgiving dinner were going to be served at any moment.

Close to the end of first stage, Claire and her husband went upstairs to their bedroom. The midwives helped with labor support. Claire's mother put her granddaughters to bed for a nap so they could be refreshed for the birth. The mother still looked peaceful, though there were a few times when it was apparent that she was struggling with the force of her contractions.

Everyone gathered in the bedroom when it was time for the birth. The younger child was still asleep in her aunt's arms, but she woke up just before the baby was born, and the expression on her face was almost as moving as the birth, "What a beautiful baby," she said. The father poured everyone a glass of champagne while the mother held her third daughter to her breast.

HELPING CHILDREN WHO ATTEND THE BIRTH

Birth is a miracle by any standard—an event that inspires wonder and awe. Seen through a child's eyes, it can be especially magical. From tiny beginnings, an unknown being grows in the mother's belly. During labor, the baby leaves this snug and warm place and makes a far more fabulous journey than could be possible on the wings of any stork. The baby travels from the secret watery depths to become part of a family, welcomed, played with, cuddled, and loved.

We can only speculate what a child really feels when witnessing a birth. By the time we translate his or her words into our adult language, the meaning is lost. A child may take it all in stride. As one physician put it, "The most beautiful births I've attended were those with children present."

Having other children at birth can help the family feel closer and more supported, and the children will better adjust to the newborn. "Oooooh look at all that blood!" or "It's worth the work to get a baby, isn't it Mom?" At the same time, a child takes nothing for granted. "Look! It's a baby! I can see the head!" "Push harder, Mom, the baby's coming!" After attending a birth, one child remarked: "He used to be a seed. Now he's my brother."

The wide-eyed look of wonder, the expression of eager anticipation, the delight, the awe, and the innocent way a child views the miracle of creation add a dimension to the birthing experience that can hardly be put into words. One physician told me that the most unforgettable births he had ever attended were those with children present. Far from interfering, he discovered, children could actually help out in a variety of ways, including bringing the parents food and singing to them. A child's laughter and casual remarks can remind the parents of the natural family-centered event that having a baby is—something that is often forgotten in the hospital environment.

An older sibling or adult should mind very young children,

of course; otherwise their own needs will go unmet, which will trouble and distract the mother during contractions. A child should be able to come and go so that he or she does not have to be cooped up in one room for an extended period of time. A birthing center or hospital with a separate play area for children is ideal. But a hospital lobby, cafeteria, and the street outside can also provide needed distraction.

All children should be prepared for the event. Preparation should include a complete explanation of labor and birth, a book with pictures, and perhaps a film. The presence and cause of blood should be discussed, as well as the sounds mothers make in labor, so that they will not come as a shock. The appearance and function of the placenta should also be explained, as this can be a surprise to a child who does not understand its purpose.

Mothers leaving unexpectedly (often in the middle of the night) and returning after a day or more with another baby can be a major emotional shock to a young child. This separation trauma can be avoided if the child attends the birth. Some people believe that a child's having attended the birth will lessen the intensity of sibling rivalry later on. If children do not attend at birth, they should certainly be brought in to visit the mother shortly afterward—and not, as is the case in many hospitals, days later. It is essential that the child incorporate the experience of having a baby and seeing the mother as early as possible.

Many parents include siblings throughout labor and birth. Sibling-attended births are becoming more common at home, at childbearing centers, and at some hospitals. Children are usually excited, enthusiastic, and glad to participate. However, they should be familiar with the birth process and well prepared (for the sight of blood and so forth) so they will know what to expect.

We had prepared our two older boys, Carl and Paul, for the birth of third child, Jonathan. However, things don't always work out as planned. When labor began, the boys happened to be visiting their grandmother for the weekend. It was the middle of the night and they arrived too late for the birth; they came just in time to watch their father cut the cord. Though they missed the best part, their faces still reflected the awe that only birth evokes.

Ideally, children should have their own support person—a friend or family member other than the birth partner. While the birth partner devotes his or her primary attention to the mother, the child's support person should do the following:

· Explain to the child what is happening, particularly when the mother vocalizes, when the head crowns, and when the placenta is delivered.
· Reassure the child that the mother's pain, grimaces, and vocalizations are normal; explain that she is working very hard to push the baby out.

· Help the child get involved by bringing food or liquids to the mother, bringing towels or hot compresses, and so forth.

· If the child prefers to sleep during most of the labor or to play in another room, be sure to call him or her just before the baby is born.

· Take the child to another room if it becomes overwhelming to watch his or her mother's labor. For example, if it is upsetting to watch the surgical repair of tears or an incision after the birth, the child can leave the room for a while and return when the procedure has been completed.

· Shortly after birth, help the child hold the baby and establish eye contact.

THE ROLE OF FRIENDS AND FAMILY AT BIRTH

Some couples invite several people to their birth—relatives, friends, children. A birth with loved ones attending can be a wonderful event for all present. Parents can invite others to share their birth in most childbearing centers, in some hospitals, and of course at home.

Sandra invited several relatives and friends to her home birth in rural Vermont. People came and left the birthing room as they pleased throughout labor. Some of them cooked a meal to be served after the birth. Two others gave active support to Sandra and her husband, Bill. During most of the labor, a few children remained in the yard playing. When the baby was almost ready to be born, all were called to witness the miracle.

Another couple, Polly and Jim, invited their parents to attend their birth, which took place in a hospital birthing room. Grandparents at birth lend a special touch to the birthing atmosphere. Besides witnessing the birth of their grandchildren, they assist their own children through the dramatic life-altering transition. Many grandparents today gave birth in the era when many women were rendered unconscious during childbirth. The grandparents are able to go through the process with their children and vicariously experience what they may have missed when they had their own babies.

The presence of familiar faces makes many women feel more secure during labor. The mother is able to experience her emotional highs and lows with those she loves and trusts. At the same time, everyone present is drawn into the dramatic events, particularly of the birth itself.

Discuss your role beforehand with the couple. They may have specific suggestions for your help, from making meals to caring for siblings:

- *Take care of your own needs.* Bear in mind that you may be up for a day and a night, perhaps longer. Bring along nutritious snacks, a sweater, a change of clothing, and mouth freshener. Wear lose, comfortable clothes.
- *Leave the couple alone from time to time, if they seem to want that.* Some mothers feel pressure to perform in the presence of others. This can cause anxiety, inhibiting labor's progress.

If she appears nervous or upset, be sensitive to her. It may be best to leave for a while.

· *Don't act as if you are in a hurry for the mother to be done with it—even if you are at times.* Labor, particularly a long one, can often be boring to an observer. If you are bored and are not integrally involved in giving support, feel free to leave and come back later.

· *Be positive.* Don't project negative fears of thoughts, as this can interfere with the mother's labor.

Your presence at birth can enhance the event for both parents—and be an experience you will always remember.

SUGGESTIONS FOR THE SECONDARY BIRTH PARTNER

Many couples invite a family member or friend to give secondary support during labor. The primary partner usually gives the essential support while the additional person helps out in many ways.

As mentioned earlier, some couples arrange for another person to give the primary support. This frees the father to do whatever he wants during labor, to share the birth with his partner emotionally, and to give forms of support that no one else can offer.

If you have never attended a birth, you will do fine and help the parents immensely if you follow the guidelines in this book. Whether or not you have attended a birth in the past, read through the entire book, paying special attention to the suggestions in this chapter. Here are some specific ways for you to help as a secondary birth partner:

- *Relieve the primary partner from time to time.* He or she may want to take breaks for meals or short naps, particularly if it is a long labor.
- *Work with the father if he is giving primary support.* For example, you may want to give the mother a back massage while the father maintains eye contact and gives her verbal encouragement through contractions. You can replenish cool washcloths for her forehead, wipe perspiration away, help her walk around, and so forth.
- *Bring the mother whatever she wants or needs*—pillows, additional washcloths, blankets. Don't hesitate to ask the staff for such things.
- *Serve the mother food and liquids.* Prepare a meal for the primary partner.
- *Be a patient advocate in the hospital.* Help the mother achieve her goals for the birth she planned. For instance, if the mother wants to avoid pain relief medication, explain that to the nurse who offers medication. Tell the nurse you will let her know if the mother changes her mind. Before talking for the mother, however, be sure you know her wishes.

- *Don't carry on idle conversation in the labor room.* This may annoy and distract the mother.
- *Look after siblings.*
- *Take photographs if the mother wants birth and/or new baby photos.* As mentioned earlier, fathers who plan to take photos during labor often forget in the excitement.
- *Help out in any other way you can.* However, *do not* take over the birth partner's role unless the mother wants you to give primary support.

WORKING WITH A TRAINED CHILDBIRTH COMPANION

There are people who attend labors for the purpose of mothering the mother and helping couples realize the details of their birth plans. Some mothers have a trained labor support person to assist in place of, or in addition to, the primary birth partner. Sometimes called labor coaches, monitrices, doulas, or childbirth companions, labor support people come from a wide variety of backgrounds. Most labor support people are maternity nurses, midwives in training, or simply laypersons who have learned to help mothers through labor on a professional basis.

Anyone, male or female, having given birth or not, can be a good support person provide that she or he has had experience at births. Workshops are held in various places to train persons interested in supporting women in labor. Most childbirth companions have special training in methods of supporting the mother and her family during labor and the postpartum period. Most are able to tailor their support to the individual mothers. Some childbirth companions provide support only during labor; others give postpartum support and breast-feeding support as well. Good childbirth companions provide emotional support for both the mother and her primary partner.

The fee for such services is usually quite reasonable ($50–$200). Often, childbirth-educators-in-training who must attend a required number of births prior to certification will attend a woman in labor for no fee.

The help of a labor support person is particularly valuable for single women, for expectant mothers whose partners are unable to attend the birth, and for couples who want an experienced person with them. A good labor support person can offer perspective, reassurance, encouragement, and suggestions. She can help with massage, comfort measures, and remain objective at times. In many ways, the support person can help husbands support their wives and give fathers as chance to take breaks. Many can also do vaginal exams to assess cervical dilation and check blood pressure and fetal heart rate.

Some couples find a trained labor support person's presence reassuring. Others find it unnecessary, interrupting their privacy and lacking any positive benefit—especially if the father is well aware of what to expect during labor and has prepared for childbirth with his partner.

A labor support person generally meets with clients during pregnancy to get to know them and learn about their goals. When labor begins, he or she accompanies them to the hospital or visits their home and remains through delivery.

Some couples hire childbirth companions if they plan to give birth in busy, understaffed, impersonal hospitals, where there can be no guarantee of continuous nursing care and where fetal monitors are the only means to monitor the baby.

The childbirth educator Henci Goer believes that all couples should consider hiring a labor support person, especially if they plan a hospital birth. "In the hospital, the doula can help the couple feel comfortable with the unfamiliar environment and be a patient advocate, seeing that their needs and wishes are respected."

Suzanne Stalls is another childbirth educator who offers labor support. She is one of three women who make up Full Circle Childbirth Services, a California-based group that offers prenatal classes, support, and post-birth discussion groups. Her services include two to four prenatal visits, depending on individual needs. At these visits, Suzanne goes over the woman's medical history, learns how the client feels about birth and her part in it, and assesses the father's involvement. She discusses the psychological, emotional, and physical realities of labor, and outlines relaxation, breathing, and guided imagery techniques so that the expectant mother is thoroughly prepared for birth.

Most of her clients give birth in hospitals. Suzanne is a patient advocate who support's a woman's right to make informed choices about her obstetrical care. She realizes that women have very different individual needs and that her role in labor is not always the same.

She recently supported a couple giving birth to their first child. The expectant mother and her husband had been married for a long time, but their pregnancy was unplanned. When they met with Suzanne, the husband was anxious about becoming a father. He doubted his ability to give his wife emotional support through labor. Suzanne's presence during labor gave him the added confidence and freedom he needed. As labor progressed, Suzanne's role become less significant; she found herself only observing the expectant father and mother working together as a team. "Watching them," she says, "was like seeing a tender, intimate love scene."

A good labor support person should be able to pull back when necessary and not be overbearing. If the woman's partner is present, it is his place to share an intimate emotional experience with her that no one else can. No sensitive support person will interfere with this role by taking over. In some situations, the expectant father and labor support person join forces to help a laboring woman feel more comfortable. For example, one woman experienced severe back labor and benefited from almost continual massage and counterpressure on her lower back for several hours. The labor support person and father-to-be both massaged her, relieving one another from time to time. While the childbirth companion was massaging, the father was able to sit by his wife's side and talk to her.

A woman or couple who want an experienced support person with them during labor should interview that person during pregnancy to get to know his or her methods. Some labor support persons are patient advocates; others are oriented toward medical intervention. It is important that parents choose a labor support person who will uphold their personal goals. Otherwise, they may find themselves working at cross-purposes during labor. A woman who plans to give birth without medication, for example, undermines her goals by hiring a support person who will prod her to take drugs at the first sign of a contraction.

The fact that someone is a childbirth instructor or a professional labor support person does not necessarily ensure their sensitivity or, for that matter, their understanding of the birth experience, as the following story shows.

On a hot day in the middle of July, a housewife in her late twenties labored in a busy Manhattan hospital. The labor support provider sat by her side. The father of the child was attuned to his wife's needs. A police officer, he had delivered two babies on emergency calls. Despite this experience, he knew little about hospital procedures or a laboring woman's feelings.

As contractions became increasingly difficult, the expectant mother wrinkled her brow and gazed at her support person with tear-filled eyes. Rather than offering encouragement, the support person, who was also a maternity nurse and childbirth educator, shook her head and said sweetly, "Would you like something?" referring to pain medication. The laboring woman's husband told the support person that his wife had planned on a natural birth.

The labor support person ignored him. She took the woman's hand and purred in her ear: "You've got to let me know what you want. I'm here to help." The laboring woman looked up with a frightened expression and asked what she could have. The labor support person offered her a choice of Demerol or epidural anesthesia.

"What is the difference?" the woman asked.

"One is a shot in the arm. The other is a needle in the back. Make up your mind and I'll return in a while."

After delivering that fantastic response, the labor support person left the room to find a doctor. I met her in the hallway and asked her what she charged for her services.

"Ninety dollars," she said.

Although this kind of professional labor support is uncommon, the story shows the need to get to know a professional labor partner carefully. She or he plays an even more dominant role than the physician, who, after all, may spend only a few moments in the birthing room while the baby is born. The labor support person will share some of the most dramatic and emotional hours in your life. You want to be sure this person supports you wholeheartedly.

If the birth partner does not have time to study this book thoroughly and learn to give effective support, a professional childbirth companion may be recommended. Unprepared fathers who have requested the services of a childbirth companion for the birth of their second child have reported that they have enjoyed the experience more than the first time.

FOR THE RELATIVE OR FRIEND WHO PLANS TO GIVE PRIMARY LABOR SUPPORT

No one can support a woman in labor quite like the man with whom she shares her life. No one else has the same relationship with her that he does. But if a woman's partner is unavailable to attend the birth or if she is single, she will need someone else to help her. No woman should go through labor alone. A trusted friend or family member can help her manage this physically overwhelming and emotionally sensitive time and contribute to a joyful birthing experience.

Anyone can learn to give effective labor support. You don't have to have given birth. Nor do you have to be a woman. Of primary importance are the desire to share the experience with the expectant mother and the willingness to do what will help her most at the time. To be an effective partner, know what to expect in labor. Be sure to view a film depicting a normal labor and birth (films are shown in most childbirth classes and are available at many libraries). A local childbirth group should be able to let you know when and where the best films are shown. If you explain that you are planning to help a woman in labor, most instructors will welcome you to view a film along with students for free or for a nominal fee.

Read this book thoroughly. Practice together the techniques described in chapters 5 and 6. Suggestions for supporting a woman in labor are similar regardless of who the labor partner is.

If possible, attend childbirth classes with the woman you will be supporting. You needn't feel out of place just because you are not the father of the child. Many women go to classes with friends or relatives. Childbirth classes will enable you to share the experience more fully and will encourage you to prepare for labor together so that you can be a greater help to her. Good, informative classes will also cover the policies of the hospital where she plans to give birth.

It is a good idea to meet the health-care provider to get to know each other before labor begins. Attending one or more prenatal exams will afford this opportunity. In any case, the physician or midwife should be informed about who will be attending the birth. You might also tour the labor and delivery unit or birthing center with the expectant mother. Meeting the nursing staff, getting familiar with the physical layout where she will be giving birth, and learning about hospital policies will allay apprehensions and contribute to a birthing environment in which you both feel more comfortable.

Discuss her feelings about medical intervention, the use of medication in labor, whether she plans to use a birthing room, to breast-feed, to leave the hospital shortly after birth, and so forth. Get to know her feelings and goals about childbirth. Don't assume she is like women you have read about in books. She has her own thoughts and fears.

Women have different ways of reacting to labor. Not all respond to the same techniques. What makes one woman feel comfortable may not be appropriate for another. Some women, for example, like to be massaged, have their hair smoothed, and their legs stroked. Others may prefer not to be touched and want verbal encouragement alone. One woman may want her labor support to distract her with conversation while another prefers silence. Some like to be told what to do from the first contraction to birth: to relax, when and how to breathe, and so forth. Some want to be informed when each contraction is halfway through and nearly finished. Some contractions are regular; you can tell when they are nearly finished by a glance at your watch or by putting one hand on her abdomen. Others don't like this sort of active coaching. They prefer a minimum of necessary instructions. Be flexible and see what is best for her.

A woman's mother can be an excellent labor partner. She both witnesses the birth of her grandchild and aids her own child through a major life transition It is a time-honored tradition in some societies for the older women who have given birth to help their daughters in labor. One physician who specializes in family-centered birth finds the births with grandmothers present particularly moving. He said, "It is a joy to see a woman's mother at a labor. Her eyes come alive as she shares the event with her daughter, crying, feeling so close, and enjoying the birth."

The mother of a laboring woman who gave birth in a medically controlled environment in the era when most women underwent general anesthesia for birth can enjoy a special privilege. As the physician quoted earlier points out: "She is able to go through the whole process with her daughter and vicariously experience what she missed when it was her turn."

Occasionally, both parents will attend the birth, or a father alone will help his daughter in labor. In one case, a man attended childbirth classes with his daughter, a single woman. He paid careful attention to everything the instructor said, but he had not attended the birth of his own two children and was at first reluctant to attend his daughter's labor. "I am only here to help Jean practice relaxation and prepare for labor," he told the other class members. "We will find another labor support person to attend the birth." But by the end of the six classes, he changed his mind. While helping his daughter prepare for birth, he became more involved than he expected. At the last class, he said: "I wouldn't miss it for the world." His daughter birthed naturally and tears streamed down the grandfather's face when the physician cut the cord.

A friend who has given birth naturally can be a most helpful support person. Only one who has had a baby herself can really understand what labor is all about. An experienced mother can reassure a laboring woman. When labor gets rough, she can say, "I know what you are experiencing. You're doing fine."

But if you have given birth, don't assume that the woman you are supporting will have a labor similar to your own. Every labor is unique. Be willing to let go of your own opinion of what childbirth should be and become involved with her experience. The best labor support person is one who steps back and puts his or her own ego aside to attune to the mother's experience.

If you are a man, don't feel that you can't give adequate labor support. Though you haven't had the benefit of going through labor and birth yourself, you can still help tremendously. Some of the finest birth attendants are men—and many are women who have never given birth.

A friend at a woman's side can work wonders during labor. But whoever the labor support person is, a positive attitude and a genuine desire to help are essential. A labor partner with a negative frame of mind can do much harm.

One single woman expecting her first child was planning to give birth naturally. She was frightened of labor and needed encouragement. A friend who was the mother of three volunteered to help her. Each of her own three labors had taken place in a large city hospital and each time she had taken much medication. When the two women attended childbirth classes together, the support person was most discouraging. During a discussion of active labor, she repeatedly warned the anxious mother how terrible labor could be and that she could never make it without medication.

In labor, the mother-to-be trembled with fear. Instead of encouraging her and trying to calm her down, her labor partner magnified her apprehension. She jabbed her in the ribs and said: "You think this is bad! This is nothing! Labor has just begun. It will get much more difficult. You'll never be able to stand it!"

This support person did no good at all. The young woman finally gave birth with the help of epidural anesthesia. She would have been better off had she shared the birth with someone else.

A labor support person—especially one who has attended several births—may share a woman's experience on an intuitive level. This phenomenon is not dissimilar to a father's sharing his partner's symptoms of pregnancy. One birth attendant who has spent many years attending both home and hospital births often experiences a tightening in his belly and a sensation he describes as "similar to menstrual cramps" shortly before a woman calls to say she is in labor. There is no scientific explanation for this phenomenon, but it happens so frequently that he has come to accept it as a probable sign that he will attend a birth within a few hours.

Helping a woman in labor can mean anything from just

sitting with her and giving encouragement to sharing her entire experience, including childbirth classes. Ideally, you and the woman you are supporting should begin preparing for labor two months or more before the due date. But if you decide to help a woman in labor at the last moment, you can still contribute to a rewarding birth experience. Even if you have done no more than read this book, your presence and help will be invaluable.

. . . .

Chapter Eleven

AFTER THE BABY IS BORN

The rapture that usually follows natural birth is a wonderful magic that's impossible to describe. The hard work is forgotten and waves of joy will probably sweep over both of you, a feeling that prompts may new parents to speak of birth and the love that follows it as holy. The new mother may feel excited, energetic, and elated, while the new father will probably feel pride, elation, tremendous excitement, and the desire to share the news of his child's birth with everyone he knows. Both parents will probably be engrossed with the baby, but it is also normal for the mother to be so exhausted that all she wants to do is sleep, and for the father to feel uncertain and dazed. Sometimes it takes a while for a woman to realize labor is over. The presence of the baby lying on her chest, skin-to-skin, is the best assurance that all is well.

THE FIRST HOURS AFTER BIRTH

The first hours after birth are a time to explore your child. If born naturally, the baby will probably be quietly alert for 1 or 2 hours before sleeping deeply for 3 or 4 hours. He or she will watch your faces intently and gaze into your eyes—a very moving experience for new parents.

Breast-feeding should be initiated within the first hour of birth when the baby is especially alert. Nursing aids maternal-infant attachment, while offering the infant a replacement for the snug, warm environment of the womb. It is also nature's way of preventing postpartum hemorrhage. When a woman nurses, the hormone oxytocin is released, causing the uterus to contract so that the blood vessels at the placental site will remain clamped shut. After the milk comes in, oxytocin sets off the "let-down reflex," the mechanism that causes the milk to be ejected into the ducts leading to the nipples. At this time, and for the first few days until the milk comes in, the breast secretion consists of colostrum, a yellowish fluid high in protein and immunity factors. Colostrum is extremely important for your newborn's system of defense against infection (especially gastrointestinal infection), and serves to cleanse his or her intestinal tract. Don't be concerned if the baby doesn't take the breast immediately. Some babies don't seem to know what to do at first but will come around eventually.

Immediately after birth the remainder of the amniotic fluid and possibly a little stream of blood will flow out of the uterus.

The uterus will contract and feel like a hard grapefruit just below the navel. The placenta separates and is delivered shortly following birth. The mother may be asked to bear down to aid its expulsion. Afterward, the placenta will be examined and stitches will be put in if there was an episiotomy or tearing. If you and your partner wish to keep the placenta for any reason, let the health-care provider know.

If the birth takes place in a hospital delivery room, the drapes covering the mother's legs and the linens under her are removed. Her legs are lowered from stirrups (if stirrups are used) and a sanitary napkin is applied. She is given a warm gown and covered in a blanket. She is then transferred to a postpartum recovery area or directly to the postpartum room.

The baby may be brought to a nursery to be weighed and measured. Drops to reduce the chance of gonococcus infection and chlamydia are placed in the baby's eyes and the baby is examined. If birth takes place in a hospital birthing room, childbearing center, or at home, the mother is cleaned up and the family usually remains together in the same room for several hours.

Your partner may experience involuntary trembling for a short spell. If so, cover her with a blanket until it stops. She can get up any time after birth as long as she takes it slowly. She should first sit up, then rise gently. Support her so she doesn't fall. When she first gets up, some blood may escape after having accumulated in the vagina. Reassure her that this is normal.

Remind her to urinate within a few hours after birth. Allowing the bladder to overfill can traumatize it and cause the uterus to be displaced, leading to the possibility of postpartum hemorrhage. She may have to sit and relax for a while before being able to urinate the first time. She may have mild to labor-like contractions for a while after birth. These "after-birth pains" are more pronounced if medication has been given to contract the uterus, after subsequent births, and during nursing. The contractions are beneficial in that they help prevent excessive postpartum bleeding. A full bladder makes it difficult for the uterus to remain contracted, so she can relieve this discomfort by urinating and lying face down with a pillow under her lower belly. The pressure will keep the uterus contracted. Afterpains may get worse in this position for a few minutes before being relieved. She can also massage the uterus, just as the nurse or midwife will do whenever they find the uterus relaxed.

UNAVOIDABLE INTERRUPTIONS

Wherever the baby is born, all routine medical procedures—weighing and measuring the baby, use of eye drops, and so forth should be delayed until after the parents and baby have had whatever time they need to interact spontaneously. These procedures can hinder the vital process of getting to know the baby, impairing the natural responses of both the parents and the child when their instincts for bonding are high.

However, the initial contact between parent and child must sometimes be interrupted or delayed. If labor was extremely long, the mother may not have the energy to interact with her child immediately after birth. If there is a medical emergency, the baby may require immediate pediatric care. Though the initial postnatal hour is important, the parents shouldn't feel worried or guilty if they are unable to remain with their baby during this time. The development of parent-infant attachment is an ongoing process.

BONDING

The first hour or so after birth is an emotionally sensitive time for parents and babies. It is a period of high energy for the new family. The new mother "takes in" her child, and the baby "takes in" her parents.

Close contact during this time enhances bonding, the beginning phase of the ongoing parent-infant attachment process. Early breast-feeding, close-range eye contact, and skin-to-skin holding all contribute positively to bonding. Studies have shown that mothers who have had prolonged contact with their infants shortly after birth demonstrate greater affection and attachment to their babies later on.

Eye-to-Eye and Skin-to-Skin Contact

When meeting his parents for the first time, the baby will usually gaze at their faces. He can best see objects that are close to his face, at the same distance from him as his mother's face when she holds him to her breast. The first moments of eye contact can be a moving, unforgettable experience. Waves of feeling swept up and down my spine when I held my first son and looked into his eyes immediately after he was born.

The mother will usually explore her newborn, first with her eyes, then her fingertips, and then enfold the baby in her arms, holding him to her, skin to skin.

The father, too, should hold the baby skin to skin. He can remove his shirt and hold the infant to his chest. A blanket over the baby's back and an infant cap on the head will provide plenty of warmth for the child.

Immediate Breast-Feeding

Ideally the mother should offer the baby the breast very shortly after birth—even if she plans to bottle-feed later. Nursing during the initial postpartum is beneficial to both baby and mother.

Benefits for the baby: The premilk substance called colostrum, secreted until the milk comes in about the first postpartum day, is rich in nutrients, vitamins, and antibodies, essential for preventing a host of illnesses. Colostrum helps to prevent infections, particularly of the intestinal tract. Immediate postpartum breast-feeding also gives the baby a feeling of security just after leaving the womb.

Benefits for the mother: Nature designed immediate post-birth nursing to be an integral part of the labor process. It assists the delivery of the placenta and helps to prevent postpartum hemorrhage in the mother.

Partners in Breast-Feeding

The partner's attitude toward nursing can spell the difference between breast-feeding success and failure. Nursing is an emotionally sensitive process. Supportive surroundings enhance milk production and let-down (milk ejection). At the same time, embarrassment, inhibitions, anxiety, or a critical mate can impair nursing by inhibiting the milk ejection reflex. Here are the basics of helping the nursing mother:

· Have a positive attitude about breast-feeding. This comes largely with learning about the subject and being involved with the mother and new baby.
· Encourage the mother to rest.
· Encourage her to drink plenty of fluids and eat a well-balanced diet.
· Support her in the presence of relatives and friends who are critical of nursing.
· Share in the feeding process by diapering and burping the baby, bringing him to the mother in the night, and staying close by while she nurses him.
· Ideally, how the baby is fed should be a joint decision by

the parents. After all, you both conceived the child and you will raise the child together. Nursing is truly satisfying only if both parents agree.

· Approach the topic of nursing together. The time to do this is during pregnancy. However, it is never too late to learn about this important subject.

· Talk to other people whose partners have nursed successfully. Read about breast-feeding. Many people who are initially opposed to nursing change their minds after learning how the entire family can benefit from breast-feeding.

Breast-feeding is the safest and most nutritious way to feed an infant, whether the child is born prematurely, by Cesarean section, or at full-term by vaginal birth. The American Academy of Pediatrics recommends breast milk as the infant's primary source of nutrition for the first six months of life. The baby will be healthier. There will be less chance of intestinal infections. The baby will have better tooth and jaw development. Many of the infant's emotional needs for cuddling and soothing talk will be met at the breast. In addition, nursing has advantages for the new family:

· There are no 2:00 A.M. bottles to prepare.
· Nursing is less expensive than bottle-feeding.
· Diapers are remarkably less odorous.

THE FIRST DAYS AND WEEKS AFTER BIRTH

During the first few exciting days following birth, the new mother is highly sensitive, vulnerable, and dependent on others for help. By meeting her physical and emotional needs, the birth partner—mate, friend, or relative—can help her make a much smoother transition to motherhood.

Helping the New Mother

In many families, the mother's mate is in the best position to offer the most help, because he lives with her and may be able to provide the intimate emotional support of shared parenting that no one else can. Additionally, a friend or relative can be an immense help to the mother, or to both parents, during the early postpartum period.

You may not have time to follow all the suggestions in this section, but any help you are able to provide during the first few days of new parenthood, when both mother and father are going through such a tremendous adjustment, will be greatly appreciated.

The birth partner's major role during the first hours after birth will probably be to celebrate and enjoy the new arrival. Here are some additional points to bear in mind:

- Be sure the room is dimly lit. If it is sunny, pull down the shades. After being in the dark environment of the womb, the newborn's eye will be sensitive for a few hours. The parents and baby will be able to enjoy eye contact only if the lights are low.

· Keep the baby warm. The newborn is not able to regulate body temperature very well. Keep the baby covered with a blanket and an infant cap. If the windows are open, close them.

· Help the mother avoid interruption. If necessary, interface with the staff and explain that the mother would like to postpone all medical procedures until she has had an hour to bond with her newborn, unless there is an emergency.

· Help the mother the first time she gets up. She can walk around as soon as she wants after birth. Help her first to sit, then rise gently. Note: some blood may escape after having accumulated in the vagina.

· Remind her to urinate within a few hours. She may not feel the need after the bladder has been jostled about during the birth process. However, allowing the bladder to overfill can traumatize the uterus and cause it to be displaced, leading to the possibility of postpartum hemorrhage.

· Take photographs if the parents want. The father is so caught up with the baby he often forgets to take photos, even if he has planned to do so in advance. If you are using a flash, be sure the parents have had time for eye contact with the baby first.

· If complications warrant immediate pediatric attention, accompany the baby and report his condition and actions to the mother later, or remain with the mother, whichever she prefers.

Tips for Fathers

Remain with the mother after birth as much as possible. If she gives birth in a hospital or childbearing center, nurses are available around the clock to give her professional help but this is no substitute for her mate. Women who give birth in hospitals are often separated from their mates after birth—at a time when they most need to be together. The mother remains in the hospital, while the father returns home alone, which many men find depressing. This custom is beginning to change as more and more parents and health professionals become aware of the importance of remaining together during this sensitive time. In some hospitals the father can remain around the clock and can room in with his mate. In most other institutions the father can come and go as he pleases and remain as long as he likes. The father is not a visitor but an integral part of the family. Couples are urged to avoid hospitals that place restrictions on the father's participation after the baby is born.

Share the baby care. Comforting the baby, clothing, changing diapers, and bathing will help you develop a relationship with your baby while giving your partner a rest. Your partner can express some breast milk into a bottle should you want to be involved in the baby's feeding, as do many fathers. If you have other children, be sure to pay attention to them. They will probably feel somewhat jealous of the new family member especially if it was a hospital birth they did not attend.

Take charge of the housekeeping and cooking. If you do not want to do all the work yourself, perhaps you can delegate responsibilities to family members and friends who offer to help. If you're doing the housework yourself, don't get so caught up with it that you have no time to be with your family.

Don't refuse offers of help. The postpartum period is no time to do everything on your own. It is quite appropriate to depend on family or friends for a few days or more.

Consider hiring a housekeeper for a few days or more to relieve the cleaning burden.

Limit excess visitors. Everyone wants to see the new baby, and most new mothers enjoy visits from friends and relatives. Too many visitors, however, can leave the mother feeling drained. If she feels tired, explain that she needs quiet time by herself to rest.

Do something special. Bring home a dinner, even if it is only a pizza. Give her a gift. Buy fresh flowers or cut them from the garden.

Let your mate know that you love her—that she is not just a maternal figure in your eyes, but that she is still attractive and interesting. Telling her "I love you, I care" is the most important form of support you can give.

Help her to breast-feed. Almost every woman who gives birth can nurse her baby. But satisfying nursing depends largely on emotional factors, as the milk ejection reflex works optimally when a woman feels relaxed, comfortable, and at ease. Help make life as easy as possible to assure a good start with breast-feeding, and encourage her to rest, drink fluids, and eat well.

Keep excess visitors at bay. Most new parents enjoy sharing their birth story with family and friends and showing off their baby. But ceaseless visits can be exhausting, especially if your partner feels she must play hostess to visitors.

Emotional ups and downs are normal during the first few days of parenthood. The new father may feel overwhelmed with his unfamiliar role, and have difficulty adjusting to new responsibilities. A husband often feels jealous or resentful of the new baby, who is getting so much love and affection from his wife. The new mother may miss her pregnancy and feel empty now that her baby is no longer a physical part of her and she no longer feels its kicks and blows. She may feel uncertain about her role as a mother. She may also feel let down when after birth the focus of attention suddenly shifts from her to her baby. Parents' feelings have to take a backseat to the baby, who needs care and attention almost all the time.

Tips for Friends and Relatives

Keep the mother company. Almost all new mothers need the reassuring presence of a loved one or friend. Your company during the first few days will be especially important if she is a single mother or if the father is unable to be present. Make her comfortable. Bring her pillows. Adjust the bed. Massage her back. Brush her hair. Keep the room quiet if she wants to rest.

Help her relieve afterpains (cramps). As mentioned before, Afterpains are labor-like cramps, ranging from mild to severe, which result when the uterus alternately relaxes and contracts. Afterpains are usually more pronounced when the mother nurses (because nursing causes the uterus to contract) and are usually worse following second and subsequent births. Suggest that the mother try to urinate. A full bladder displaces the uterus and prevents it from remaining contracted. Suggest that she lie in a prone position (belly down) with a pillow under her lower abdomen. This puts pressure on the uterus and causes it to remain contracted. Cramps may intensify for a short while, then be completely relieved.

Assist with baby care. If the mother is in bed, bring the baby to her for feedings. Change diapers, help her bathe and dress the newborn. However, do not take over baby care. To best adjust to their new role the mother or parents should take on the major share of newborn care.

Help out around the house. Do the cooking, cleaning, shopping, laundry—whatever you have time for. If you are stopping in now and then to visit the mother (rather than staying with her for several days), bring her a home-cooked meal or take-out food.

Baby Blues

Many new mothers experience "baby blues" beginning sometime between the third and fifth postpartum day. Exhaustion, hormonal changes following birth, physical discomforts such as soreness from stitches, and the emotional changes accompanying new parenthood are contributing causes. You can help your partner reduce the chance of after-birth blues by helping her through a natural birth and remaining with her the first few days postpartum. Discussing the responsibilities of new parenthood during pregnancy will also help to prepare you both, so that the inevitable change of lifestyle is not such a sudden shock.

The expression "baby blues" refers to a group of negative emotions (including tears, irritability, and depression) that the mother experiences around the third or fifth day after the birth. The "blues" may continue from one day to several weeks and may range from a vague "down" feeling to inexplicably low spirits and frequent crying. Baby blues is sometimes called "postpartum depression," but this is not to be confused with clinical depression, which requires professional care.

There are several conflicting factors—hormonal changes, mother's sudden change in life-style, the sudden confrontation of a new and irreversible role, and perhaps physical discomforts. Some believe that the blues is a normal and practically inevitable part of new motherhood. This is a myth.

But this trauma can be minimized if the mother and baby remain together (room in) throughout their hospital stay, and, when the mother and baby are healthy, by an early discharge (going home 6 to 24 hours after birth). The latter enables the woman to integrate the experience of new motherhood in her home setting.

The father is also apt to become depressed or feel a real let-down in returning to an empty home after the excitement of birth. In most medical institutions fathers are permitted to visit their partners and newborns whenever they want day or night. Still, this does not replace remaining together. Health professionals are beginning to recognize and allow for the emotionally sensitive time of new parenthood. At a few hospitals fathers are welcome to remain with their families throughout the postpartum stay—an extra bed is brought right into the room—which is the way it should be.

Post-birth blues are significantly less common after home births. This is presumably because a woman is not moved to an unfamiliar environment during such a sensitive time and because birth at home is welcome as a natural event rather than a medical crisis. At home the woman remains with her family. Her baby is born in the place where it will live. Leaving her familiar and secure home during labor, giving birth in an impersonal medical environment, having her baby removed for several hours—as is the case with a central nursery—and returning home, one, two, or more days later with a baby in her arms is bound to be an emotional trauma for any woman.

One British study showed that 60 percent of mothers who gave birth in hospitals suffered from baby blues, while only 16 percent who gave birth at home had the blues. This doesn't imply that the mother must have a home birth to avoid the blues. But it does imply that her environment has a profound impact on her emotions after birth. Talk with the mother about her feelings, particularly if she has had a disappointing birth experience.

Don't minimize her difficulty. A nurturing, caring presence in the days that follow birth will not necessarily eliminate the blues, but it can make life seem much brighter to the new mother. If the blues persist past several weeks, or if they are very severe, consult the mother's health-care provider or prenatal instructor for advice.

PHYSICAL AND EMOTIONAL CHANGES

Giving birth is a life-altering event for both parents. You will need time to put it in perspective. The new father should realize that a woman's emotional experience of her labor and birth are often quite different from his. Her feelings and reactions have a lot to do with the fact that the baby came from her body. She may feel temporary grief over the "loss of her pregnancy," along with difficulty in adjusting to the reality of the baby outside her womb.

Sometimes the mother's feelings may not seem reasonable to you. Your understanding will mean a lot. At first the new mother will probably feel energetic, elated. The new father will probably be flooded with pride and joy. And the new baby will probably be especially alert for an hour or so before falling into a deep sleep.

Don't be concerned, however, if the mother does not feel elated and immediately in love with her newborn. If there have been complications, if labor has been overlong, or if pain relief or other medications have been used, she may feel so exhausted that all she wants to do is sleep, and the father may feel dazed and uncertain for a while. After a very long labor one new mother said, "I was utterly wiped out after Kristen was born. All I wanted was to be left alone to sleep."

The mother's entire body undergoes dramatic changes beginning after labor. The most obvious takes place in the reproductive organs and breasts. The uterus gradually begins to return to its nonpregnant shape. As this occurs, excess material from the uterine walls is eliminated by means of a vaginal discharge called lochia, which is bright red for about three days, shades to pink or brown until around the tenth day, then becomes almost colorless or yellowish. Too much activity, or a problem such as a retained placental fragment, may cause the lochia to continue to be bright red or revert to red once it has become pink or colorless. If this occurs, the mother should take it easy and consult her health-care provider without delay.

For the first few days, the breasts secrete colostrum. About the second or third day, the milk "comes in." At this time the breasts may become swollen and uncomfortable for 24–48 hours, whether or not the mother is nursing. The best way to alleviate this is feeding the baby "on demand," that is, whenever he cries for milk.

She may be uncomfortable. As one new mother put it, "The bottom, the boobs, the head—all were hurting." The perineal area (around the genitals and anus) will probably be especially sore, particularly if the mother has had an episiotomy or has torn during birth. Though she can be up and about any time she wants after birth, she does require rest, especially during the first week or so. Plenty of rest is essential for both her physical and emotional recovery.

Emotional up and downs and mood swings are common during the days and weeks following birth. A woman's life is irreversibly transformed. She is now a mother 24 hours a day, seven days a week. All of a sudden she is responsible for a vulnerable, tiny being who is utterly dependent on her. The responsibility may sometimes be overwhelming—especially when she's been up in the middle of the night with a crying baby. Conflicting feelings are to be expected. The mother may feel overjoyed at one moment, at another she may resent the baby, then feel guilty for having felt this way. She is bound to feel awkward and insecure about infant care at first. Confidence comes with experience.

PATERNITY LEAVE

Every new father should seriously consider taking a week's paternity leave or more to be with his new family. Even if it seems awkward and inconvenient, the time you take off will be well worth the effort. As one new father recalls: "I would never have considered taking a week off if my wife had not told me how important it was to her. The guys at work gave me a hard time about it at first. But when I told them how important this week meant to me and my family, they changed their tune. Now that it's their turn to become fathers, some of them are doing the same thing themselves!"

Ken, a physician in training, took a leave of absence after the birth of his daughter, His wife, Laura, recalls, "Knowing he was right there when I was forging a new identify was the most valuable help of all."

In the words of Dr. David Stewart, executive director of The National Association of Parents and Professionals for Safe Alternatives in Childbirth (NAPSAC), "Fatherhood is the ultimate of manhood. Being a father is the one thing that only a man can do. Take pride in it and apologize to no one for giving your time and first consideration to your family, sometimes putting your job second."

Although you will probably not be paid for the time you take off (most men aren't, unless they have vacation time they can use), the benefits of paternity leave will more than outweigh the financial loss:

· You will find it easier to adjust to your new role as father.
· You will have some uninterrupted time to develop an intimate bond with your child.
· You will be able to catch up on much needed rest.
· You will be able to give your mate emotional support.
· You will be able to help out around the house.

After their first child was born, David remained with his wife, Sharon, both in the hospital and later at home. Sharon recalls, "If the baby woke up and wasn't hungry, David would hold him, rock him, and change him. This gave me a chance to take much needed naps."

Another mother says, "Rod stayed home for a few days after our daughter was born. Though he didn't do much around the house, his presence made all the difference to me. It made me feel secure and helped me take on my new role at a time when I felt the need of mothering myself."

Taking paternity leave is invaluable even if there are others available to help out around the house and meet the mother's practical and emotional needs. Your presence is needed to help both of you better cope with the realities of shared parenthood.

THE FATHER'S NEEDS

One of my colleagues once remarked, "New parents tend to first fulfill the needs of the person who screams the loudest.

Usually that's the baby." Siblings and the new mother are often tied for second place. But, the new father has needs, too.

Though you are not the main support-giver during the early postpartum, it does not mean you must be The Rock of Gibraltar. You may experience many of the same emotional changes that the mother does. After all, you, too, have crossed the one-way bridge to parenthood. Your life, too, is changing. If you are like most new fathers, you will probably need your mate as much as she needs you.

Anton, one new father, recalls, "I was overwhelmingly excited in the hospital. Two days later, when we brought the baby home and he was up crying half the night, I realized—here the baby was planted on us and we didn't know what to do with him!"

Many feel jealous of the new baby who gets so much love and affection. You may feel you are taking a backseat to the baby for a while. Getting involved with the baby and spending time with your new family can help you feel more like an integral part of things.

Meanwhile, you will no doubt want to be reassured that you are not being displaced by the newcomer. Most new fathers need to know that they still have their mate's attention and affection, that they are still loved, still desired. Though you should be understanding and considerate of your mate's emotional up and downs, you should not ignore your own needs, particularly as the weeks pass.

Discuss your feelings with your mate. Set aside some time for each other—just by yourselves if you feel the need. Go out to dinner, to a movie, for a walk. Support one another during this life-transforming time. From time to time, both parents may need to be reminded that having a baby is not the end of romance but a new dimension in their shared love.

ABOUT THE AUTHOR

Carl Jones is a certified childbirth educator who has attended hundreds of births and organizes childbirth workshops nationally. He lives in Whitefield, New Hampshire.

.

Notes

Notes

Notes

Notes

Notes

Notes

Notes

Notes

Notes

Notes